CAMBRIDGE LIBRARY COLLECTION

Books of enduring scholarly value

Travel and Exploration

The history of travel writing dates back to the Bible, Caesar, the Vikings and the Crusaders, and its many themes include war, trade, science and recreation. Explorers from Columbus to Cook charted lands not previously visited by Western travellers, and were followed by merchants, missionaries, and colonists, who wrote accounts of their experiences. The development of steam power in the nineteenth century provided opportunities for increasing numbers of 'ordinary' people to travel further, more economically, and more safely, and resulted in great enthusiasm for travel writing among the reading public. Works included in this series range from first-hand descriptions of previously unrecorded places, to literary accounts of the strange habits of foreigners, to examples of the burgeoning numbers of guidebooks produced to satisfy the needs of a new kind of traveller - the tourist.

Old Highways in China

In 1873, the Christian missionary Isabelle Williamson set out from Chefoo (Yantai), China, to spread the gospel to Chinese women. Her four separate journeys along the ancient roads of Shandong Province and Beijing are recorded in *Old Highways of China* (1884), a chronicle of the everyday lives of the women to whom she preached. 'My interest was chiefly in the women', Williamson explains, 'and I looked at all through a woman's eyes'. Reserving her missionary work for another publication, Williamson devotes this keenly observed book to the details of life in the villages she visited—the work, play, rituals, and stories of women and girls. It also describes Williamson's own remarkable travels, set against the stunning natural backdrop of northern China. An important witness to women's missionary work in China, her book is also testament to the intelligent eye of its author as she seeks to portray 'China's daughters'.

T0370881

Cambridge University Press has long been a pioneer in the reissuing of out-of-print titles from its own backlist, producing digital reprints of books that are still sought after by scholars and students but could not be reprinted economically using traditional technology. The Cambridge Library Collection extends this activity to a wider range of books which are still of importance to researchers and professionals, either for the source material they contain, or as landmarks in the history of their academic discipline.

Drawing from the world-renowned collections in the Cambridge University Library, and guided by the advice of experts in each subject area, Cambridge University Press is using state-of-the-art scanning machines in its own Printing House to capture the content of each book selected for inclusion. The files are processed to give a consistently clear, crisp image, and the books finished to the high quality standard for which the Press is recognised around the world. The latest print-on-demand technology ensures that the books will remain available indefinitely, and that orders for single or multiple copies can quickly be supplied.

The Cambridge Library Collection will bring back to life books of enduring scholarly value (including out-of-copyright works originally issued by other publishers) across a wide range of disciplines in the humanities and social sciences and in science and technology.

Old Highways in China

ISABELLE WILLIAMSON

CAMBRIDGE
UNIVERSITY PRESS

CAMBRIDGE UNIVERSITY PRESS

Cambridge, New York, Melbourne, Madrid, Cape Town, Singapore,
São Paolo, Delhi, Dubai, Tokyo

Published in the United States of America by Cambridge University Press, New York

www.cambridge.org
Information on this title: www.cambridge.org/9781108015189

© in this compilation Cambridge University Press 2010

This edition first published 1884
This digitally printed version 2010

ISBN 978-1-108-01518-9 Paperback

CHINESE PEASANT LIFE—GOING TO MARKET.

(*From a Chinese Engraving.*)

OLD HIGHWAYS IN CHINA

BY

ISABELLE WILLIAMSON

OF CHEFOO, NORTH CHINA

THE RELIGIOUS TRACT SOCIETY

56 PATERNOSTER ROW, AND 65 ST PAUL'S CHURCHYARD

1884

LONDON : PRINTED BY
SPOTTISWOODE AND CO., NEW-STREET SQUARE
AND PARLIAMENT STREET

PREFACE.

DURING my earlier years, in the company of my husband, Dr. Williamson, I made several journeys through the province of Cheh-kiang, and resided in some of the cities in the interior of that province. At that time I gave my impressions of the women of China in a series of articles, entitled 'Our Sisters in China.' These appeared in the 'Leisure Hour' for 1863.

In 1864, removing to the province of Shan-tung, which had been recently opened to foreigners, I occupied myself for some years in tentative work in Chefoo and the neighbourhood. After becoming familiar with the language of that district, and also with the habits and etiquette of the women of that province, I made four long journeys, two of which are briefly described in the following pages.

The first journey was undertaken in the autumn of

1873, *viâ* Weihien, Tsi-nan-foo, Tai Shan, and the cities
of Confucius and Mencius, returning by Mung, Yiu hien,
and Tsingchow-foo; the second in 1875 to Weihien,
Tsi-nan-foo, and back; the third in 1881 from Chefoo
to Peking, as narrated; the fourth in the spring of
1882, partly on the ' Old Highways,' and partly on the
byways and bridle-paths of the eastern portion of
Shan-tung.

The object of these journeys was first to carry
Gospel truth to as many of the women of China as
I could reach, and secondly, to familiarise them with
Western women, and so to render the visits of those
who followed me more easy.

Both objects were attained, and the result has been
that Western women can safely travel and reside in any
part of the province.

This volume does not profess to give an account of
mission work—that will be found in our denominational
literature—but rather records observations of every-day
life made during my journeys through North China
and during my intercourse with the people.

I trust, however, that it will deepen the interest of
English readers in the women of China; they well
deserve it. As regards natural endowments, they
are, as may be supposed, in every respect compeers

of the men—active, intelligent, and, like our sisters in every land, more open to religious teaching than the men are.

Missionaries of the widest information and greatest experience, both in China and India, concur in affirming that missionary operations have reached that point when efficient zenana work is indispensable to satisfactory progress. They find that men will never be converted in any large numbers till the women are won over to the side of Christianity. The women conserve the ancient religions and superstitions of their country ; and what can a man do when the women of the household are against him ? The elevation, therefore, of the nations of the East, and the advancement of Christianity among them, depend to a large extent upon the women of Christendom.

Again, the promises of Scripture converge towards the Gospel being preached to every creature. Nearly half the women of the world belong to the two great empires of China and India. The Scriptures can never be fulfilled so long as these Eastern women have not had even the opportunity of hearing of the Gospel of Salvation. The end of all evils, therefore, and the fulfilment of the purposes of God, seem contingent on our Zenana work. I look upon work among the women of the East as now the great question of the Christian Church.

There are many noble-minded women of independent means and few family ties wishing for an outlet equal to their zeal, and why should they not go forth resolved to spend their lives in this work ? In such a beautiful country as North China there is no more danger to health than there is in the Northern States of America or in Australia.

May God so bring home, to those who can go, the needs of the women of China, that there may soon be a great going forth of the Christian women of Great Britain, thus fulfilling the prophecy contained in Psalm lxviii. 11, new version : ' The Lord giveth the word, and the women that bring glad tidings are a great host.'

ISABELLE WILLIAMSON.

CONTENTS.

—⋈—

CHAPTER I.

CHAPTER V.

CHAPTER VI.

CHAPTER VII.

CHAPTER VIII.

CHAPTER IX.

CHAPTER X.

CHAPTER XV.

CHAPTER XVI.

CHAPTER XVII.

CHAPTER XVIII.

CHAPTER XIX.

CHAPTER XX.

CHAPTER XXI.

CHAPTER XXII.

CHAPTER XXIII.

CHAPTER XXIV.

CHAPTER XXV.

ILLUSTRATIONS.

———◆◇◆———

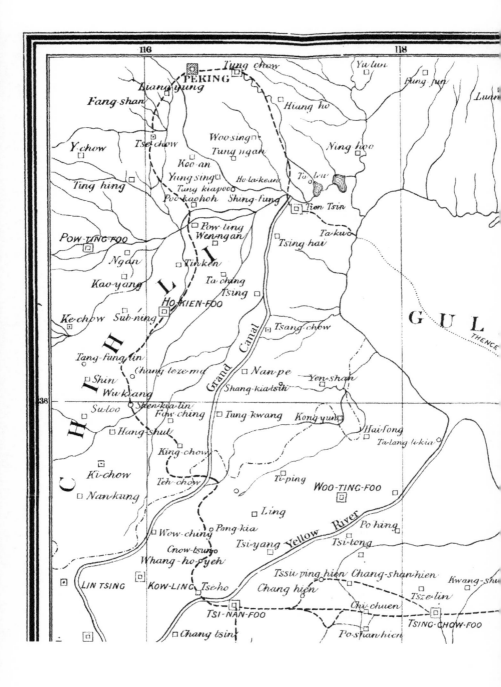

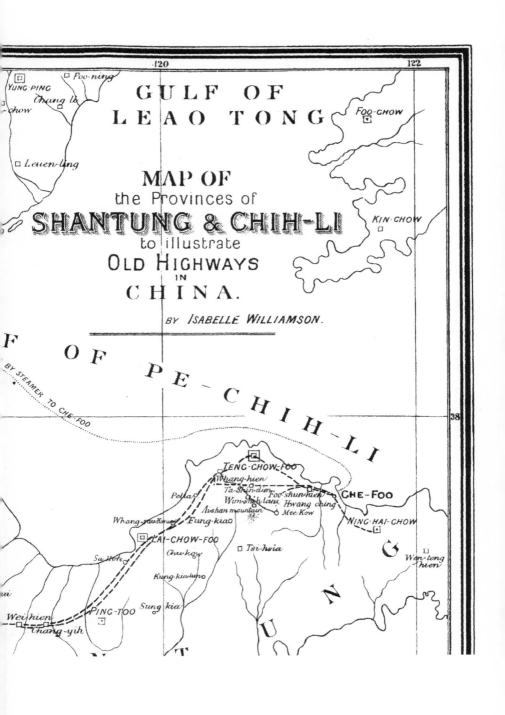

GULF OF
LEAO TONG

MAP OF
the Provinces of
SHANTUNG & CHIH-LI
to illustrate
OLD HIGHWAYS
IN
CHINA.

BY ISABELLE WILLIAMSON.

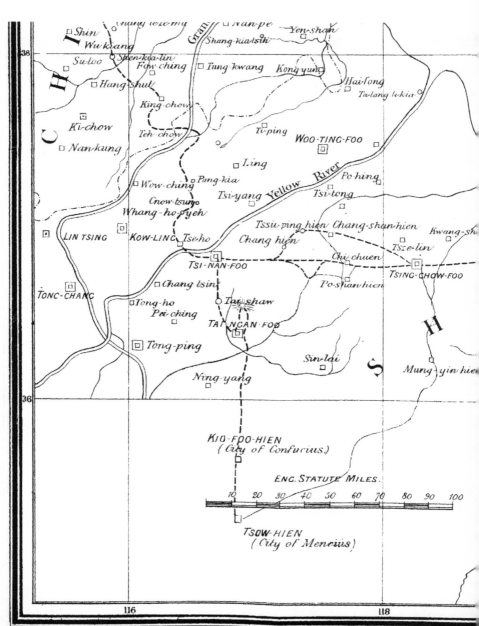

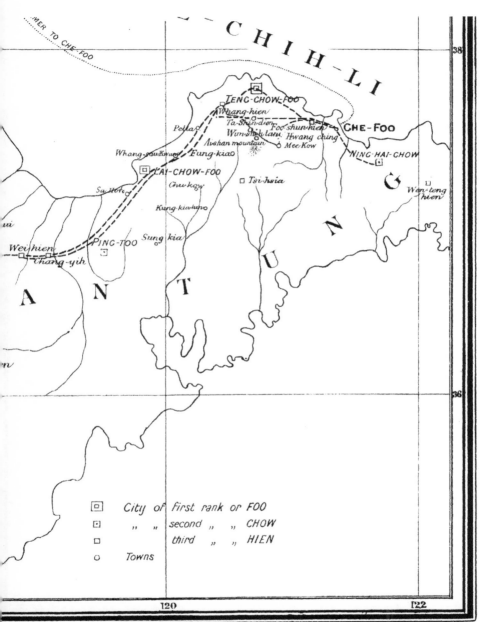

STEAMER TO CHE-FOO

CHIH-LI

TENG-CHOW-FOO

Whang-hien

Ta-shun-dien

Pella

Wun-shih-lau

Whang-chow-kwang

Avshan mountain

Foo-shun-hien

CHE-FOO

Hwang-ching

Mee Kow

Eung-kiao

NING-HAI-CHOW

Whang-chow-kwang

LAI-CHOW-FOO

Chu-kay

Tsi-hsia

Wen-teng-hien

Sa Hok

Kung-kia-hwo

Sung-kia

Wei-hien

PING-TOO

Chang-yih

A   N   T   U   N   G

□ City of first rank or FOO

⊡   „   „   second „   „ CHOW

□   third   „   „ HIEN

○   Towns

120   122

G. PATERNOSTER BUILDINGS E.C.

A CHINESE BULLOCK CART ON A COUNTRY ROAD.

OLD HIGHWAYS IN CHINA.

CHAPTER I.

Old highways—Their great interest, antiquarian and modern—
China's daughters — Our vehicles — Their construction and
motion—Our start—Our travelling companions, their dress and
idiosyncrasies.

FROM Chefoo to Peking is a journey of about seven
hundred miles, and we go by the Old Highways.

Old Highways indeed! old, almost beyond historical
record. Trodden by the feet of more than a hundred
generations, they are yet fresh as of yore, and ever and
anon present landscapes of the rarest beauty. To one

acquainted with the language and habits of the people
these highways are a never-ending book of antiquity,
from which to read the story of the past, blended with
the life thoughts of the present. China comes to us
like a submerged continent newly upheaved from the
ocean of time; and on its vast extent there are no
objects of interest greater than China's daughters.
Beautiful they are with a certain beauty of their own.
On them, alas! centuries of non-culture have pressed
heavily; but now, Undine-like, each Chinese maid and
matron seems rising and asking for a soul.

On the journey my interest was chiefly in the
women, and I looked at all through a woman's eyes.

April 7th is the day fixed for our start.   The
muleteers promise to be in good time; all arrangements
have been made, and nothing has to be done in the
morning but to load the animals.

Our preparations have not been extensive, as we
depend on native sources for our supplies. We take
a few pounds of sugar, a pound or so of tea, four tins
of condensed milk, a small bag of sea biscuit, three
bottles of arrowroot, a few articles of crockery, and a
small medicine chest.   Our clothing is in a carpet sack,
which serves for a pillow. A dressing bag does a like
duty.   These, and a Chinese quilt for each, comprise
our travelling outfit.

There is a small mountain of books to be conveyed,
inasmuch as to sell and distribute good books is one of
the main objects of our journey. They also are piled
up in readiness.

Mules are always used for long journeys, as they
are hardy and sure-footed. True to their promise, at
early dawn the muleteers lead the mules into our

courtyard. To convey our books and baggage we require six animals. They are all examined to see that they are in good condition. One mule has a large wooden pack-saddle; a second has a pair of immense panniers.

Our vehicles are called shendzles, and each shendzle requires two mules. These shendzles are of the simplest construction, and are very light. Three small wooden pack-saddles are laid on the ground about three feet apart. These are fastened to two poles about eighteen feet long. After the poles are securely tied to the upturned saddles, three narrow but strong strips of bamboo are arched over the poles. Reed matting is spread upon the bamboos, and sewn firmly to them with twine. Betwixt the poles, about two feet from either end, there is stretched a broad band of cowhide. The shendzle mules have wooden pack-saddles, and in the centre of each saddle is fixed an iron spike, standing upright. In the middle of the band of untanned cowhide a hole is pierced, and in putting the shendzle on the backs of the mules, the poles are raised so high that the iron spike on the saddle can be run through the hole in the cowhide band. There is no strap or fastening. There you are—balanced. Very careful driving is required, and a good muleteer is always on the watch to lay hold of the poles at any signs of toppling.

Over the shendzle we tied a sheet of vulcanised indiarubber cloth, which is most useful in travelling. It defends from both sun and rain. Every night it is spread on the sleeping-place, as a protection from damp, and in very many other circumstances it is a comfort.

Our energetic friend, Mr. Paton, looks after the packing of the books. The panniers are filled with

them. A box of them is strapped on each side of the
pack-saddle, and the remainder is packed away in the
under parts of the shendzles. Our quilts and eatables
are put in. Everything being ready, we are invited to
crawl into the place that is to be a home for many days.

We crawl in. Good-byes are said to numerous
teachers and Chinese friends. All the school girls and
boys and all the members of the establishment come
up and wish us a good journey and a speedy return.
We say good-bye to Mr. Paton, and to the sunny-haired
English baby in the arms of her smiling mother. How
fair and sunny the two look beside the bronzed and
yellow-tinted sons and daughters of China !

Well, of all vehicles a shendzle is one of the fun-
niest. Outwardly, it looks like a gigantic chrysalis ;
inwardly, it seems comfortable as a couch. There is
great difficulty in the balancing of it. Slung simply
on the backs of the mules, an unlucky, awkward movement of the traveller within it may send it rolling down
the first precipice. So soon as we are fairly started,
one is requested to sit ' a little more to the north ' ;
then, ' a little more to the south ' ; ' no, not so much ' ;
till, after a variety of orders and counter-orders, at last
the muleteer is satisfied. We climb a hill immediately
after starting, and we soon find that the mules have
had no training, and never by any chance step together.
We are rocked from side to side cradle fashion, then
jolted to and fro from head to heel.

Backwards, forwards, see-saw, zig-zag, jerk, jolt,
jog, joggle !—the proverbial ' baby on the tree top ' must
have had quiet compared to this.

Sea-sickness is disagreeable, but *mal de shendzle* is
worse. However, the disagreeable experience usually

passes away with one day; and it is found that, although
it is a very unsocial, yet it is not an altogether unpleasant, mode of travel. Few can read in a shendzle,
and those who do read must have books of very large
type. A Chinese book in good-sized type may be read
with comfort.

Our travelling companions are two muleteers, a help
for bookselling, and a man who is half servant half man
of business. My muleteer, who claims the lead, is a roguish
looking man, rather surly and taciturn. He has some
ugly scars on his visage, and a peculiar leer in one eye.
He is strong and hardy, and has the reputation of being
a perfect walking map. His head is adorned with a
marvellous cap of soft grey felt. On ordinary days it
looks like a plain skull-cap. As the weather changes I
discover that this cap is a *multum in parvo*. If the
wind blows hard from the north, he immediately doffs
his cap, and pulls out a flap that defends his ear and
neck. If the mornings are cold, the cap has flaps to
cover both ears. Should the sand be driving in his face,
an immense scoop is projected in front to protect his
eyes. When it rains, a great peak appears, to prevent the
water running in at the collar of his jacket. His jacket
is of blue cotton, wadded. His continuations are buff-
coloured leather. He has white cotton stockings quilted
with cotton, and black cloth shoes with a most liberal
allowance of sole. He carries a whip at his girdle, but,
to my great comfort, seldom uses it. The other muleteer
is a younger man, with a quiet look. He is dressed
much in the same style—only his continuations are of
olive-green leather, and he is not the proud possessor
of a *multum in parvo* cap.

The bookseller was engaged the evening before we

started. He was recommended as a 'decayed gentleman.' He is very much decayed indeed, but he has a cheery, happy-go-lucky way, and is not an unpleasant travelling companion. He has a faculty of making friends, not enemies. We were obliged to take him in the place of a dear old man who became ill just before we left, and who died ere we returned from our journey.

The man Friday is a fine, tall, handsome Chinaman, a good scholar, and a gentleman in his manners. He can do anything, from writing a Chinese document to boiling an egg, and he has a marvellous facility for making palatable whatever provisions we can get at inns or country markets. He is the butt of the party. His mounting on his mule is one of the sights not to be lost. Many directions he receives as to his demeanour on his steed. 'Sit to the east,' is shouted to him ; again, 'To the west'—'More to the back'—'Nearer to the front'—and he makes an effort to comply as far as he can. His perch is on the mule with the panniers, and he falls off on an average three times a day. It is supposed that he goes to sleep, and thus overbalances the panniers. His falls are not serious, as the panniers save him, and he is generally found seated in one of them. He always persists in packing the crockery in these panniers, as a proof that he has no fear of an upset, but after reducing us to one teacup, he becomes exceedingly careful to put it in the snuggest place in my shendzle. I fear I must be troublesome to him, as I constantly tease him to read all the sentences the Chinese write on their doors, and also the ornamental scroll-work with which they decorate their dwellings. He is a most agreeable companion, and never loses his temper : his wits he sometimes loses.

CHAPTER II.

Our first halting-place—An old friend and his family—Hearty welcome and cordial greetings—How mandarins become rich—The
famous mountain, Ai-Shan—Legendary lore—A quaint and
beautiful story pertaining to Ai-Shan.

OUR path lay off the main road and through a fine
valley. The greater part of the way was a watercourse,
lined on each side with lovely trees.

We had arranged to stay the first night at the house
of one of our church members, a faithful old man with
small ability but a true heart. He and his friends were
expecting our visit. As we emerged from the shade of
the trees, and were crossing a stony ridge at the head
of the glen, in the dim twilight, we could descry figures
and hear voices hailing us, and shouting, 'Take the
north road.' Presently we met the old man and his
son, their faces beaming. In the distance we could see
lights and hear the hum of a village.

As we got near to the house, just on the edge of the
hamlet, we found nearly all the villagers assembled.
The greetings were numerous and cordial. Women
came round, and were introduced as the mothers of sons
named to us. Indeed, a woman's title in China is usually
the name of her eldest son; and what title is sweeter to
a mother's ear?

Everything was made tidy for us. The best *kang* [1]

----

[1] Brick bed.

was lit, and the mill-room arranged for a sitting-room. For a long time Dr. Williamson sat conversing with the men on religious subjects. In the inner room, entering by another door, I saw the women. It was pleasant to find how much of Scripture truth the women and girls knew.

The family of our host consisted of his wife, a son, and a daughter, the brightest little Chinese maiden I have ever seen. She was greatly interested in my buttoned boots; the particular fault of this little Chinese maid was a tendency to be untidy in her gaiters and shoes. So she at once informed her mother that she would not need to be scolded for her besetting sin if her shoes and gaiters were all in one piece, as mine were, and if they were made of leather. Altogether she took my heart—a cheery, sunny, little lassie.

The story of this family is a good illustration of how an unjust magistrate may oppress his people. Some five or six years ago this man had, in foreign employment, saved about one hundred and twenty thousand cash. For a peasant this is quite a little fortune. The mandarin of the district, a very petty magistrate indeed, knew this. For some time he sought an occasion to bring this man up before him on some offence. First he had him arraigned on a charge of having broken down a small mud embankment, and sent water and stones over a field belonging to a neighbour. But it was clearly proved that the water and stones had found their way into that field without Shoo's help. At the time of the floods the man was at his work in Chefoo, some twenty miles away; and his wife could not have walked such a distance in the storm. This charge thus fell to the ground, though a horde of underlings had to

be paid their fees. Nevertheless the mandarin raised
another case against him, and kept it on and on, till,
by fines and otherwise, he got the one hundred and
twenty thousand cash Shoo had saved. He then released
his victim, who had all the costs of the suit to pay.
Old and poor, he has to begin again ; and he says, ' If I
save any money now, I'll be careful not to let my
neighbours know.'

A CHINESE OFFICIAL.

There is nothing a respectable Chinaman fears
more than to get into the clutches of the mandarins.
He prefers to suffer loss rather than go to law to
recover a debt, particularly if he has any money to
lose.

After a comfortable night, and after seeing a great
many Chinese who were clamouring around us before

sunrise, we started from Mee Kow about seven A.M.
Almost immediately on leaving Shoo's village, afar on
the horizon, framed in by the arching trees, rises on our
view the lofty Ai-Shan. Its summit is strikingly like
the dome of St. Paul's, but under a bluer sky. The
general outline of the whole mountain is suggestive of
a majestic cathedral. Its highest peak is seen afar
off on the sea by the mariner, and guides him into
harbour.

The following is a legend of this mountain :—

A young girl, beautiful and affectionate, lived under
the shadow of the celebrated Ai-Shan. Her father
owned property in junks, and was very rich. She had
two brothers older than herself. Her father and her
two brothers set sail for the south, one fine autumn day.
They went each in charge of a junk. The girl was
sorry to part with them; but they comforted her by
promising to return in the following summer, when the
soft south wind would waft them gently home to their
own quiet bay, and they would bring beautiful presents
for her, as by next autumn she would be wearing the
scarlet dress of a bride.

Months passed, and the young maiden dwelt with
her mother. When the winter wind howled round
their home at night, she used to shiver, as she thought
of her dear father and brothers in the junks, tossing on
the stormy sea. Sometimes an old friend of her father
would come to visit them. This man was also rich, and
a junk owner. The fair young maiden sat inside the
damask embroidered curtains, and listened to the tales
of the sunny south which the old junk owner was in
the habit of telling her mother. Inside the curtain she
sat because it was not etiquette for her to be seen; but

the old man knew that she was a far more attentive listener than the old mother, who would interrupt him in his most lovely description by asking if her husband was sure to make lots of money. The old man loved the girl, whom he seldom saw, for he hoped to have her for a daughter-in-law. His only child, a son, was with the junks.

Winter with its storms passed over ; spring came ; then summer, and the gentle south wind, that was to waft the dear ones home, died in the changing monsoon.

Day by day preparation was made for the return of the sailors. Daily Ahn Yune longed to be able to go up the Ai-Shan just a little way, to see the ocean where sailed the loved ones, but was prevented by Chinese etiquette. Another summer was passing away. Still the junks came not. Night after night she dreamt of her father and brothers, still they came not. Summer also had its storms, with lashing rain, and dreadful thunder, and lightning flashing into her chamber.

One night she dreamt a dream. In the morning she was found lying on her *kang*. Her garments were dripping, her hair was dank with sea-water, and she lay pale and exhausted. They changed her clothing and carried her to her mother's *kang*. There she revived, and then she told her dream :—

' I went up Ai-Shan, oh ! so far—high up amid the clouds. Then I saw the sea, and away off, just like three specks, the three junks. Suddenly the clouds gathered black, the thunder rolled, and under each lightning flash I saw the junks, the sea beating over them. They could not reach the harbour, for the wind was in their teeth ; the black rocks were behind them ; they dared not go back. Suddenly I felt myself moving near to them. I came so near that I saw my father's face and the faces of my brothers. They were all imploring Heaven to save them. "Heaven has sent me," I said; but they heeded not, for they did not see me. On my father's junk I saw one, young and handsome, I knew, though I had never seen him; that was *he*, and I loved him. One brother's junk was on the right side of my father's, the other on the left side. Down into the cold dashing sea I went, laid hold by one hand of my eldest brother's junk cable, and with the other my younger brother's junk. Then I said, "Oh! my father!" And lo! I felt something across my mouth. With my teeth I grasped the cable of my father's junk. Then we sailed straight for Ai-Shan. I could not turn my head, but I felt the three junks towing after me. Something whispered, "Trust in Heaven, do not be afraid." We sailed swiftly on. Waves dashed—I was not afraid. Thunder rolled—I was not afraid. We sailed so close to land I could only see the peak of Ai-Shan. Closer, and I could not see Ai-Shan. The sea washed my hair; the silver pin became detached; it fell down my back. I opened my mouth to say, "Oh! my silver pin!" for I was vain of it. The cable slipped from my teeth. I lost my father's junk. In a second my brothers' junks touched land. I sprang on a rock, to see where my father's junk had gone. Oh! horrors! it was sticking on a great black rock. In the front stood my father, and that other, and I loved him. The great waves broke over them; the foam covered all. Again the masts shook, the foam dashed. I saw the two; the young man held the old man in his arms. Again the foam broke, but only over the rock; the great junk was not there. I sped home, and the day dawned.'

'Let us get down to Chefoo,' was on every tongue.
'Yes, I can lead you to the place.'

Litters, mules, donkeys are fast carrying them to
Yentai, the port of Chefoo. The old junkman heads the
cavalcade; straight towards the harbour sands they go.
Ahn Yune rises up in her litter. 'There are the two
junks,' she cries, 'and yonder the black jagged rocks.
Oh! my father!'

On they go. The junks are there. A crowd is on
a rock. Two handsome, stalwart men are wringing
their hands. An old and handsome man lies there, just
washed up by the sea, and by his side a young and
noble-looking man. 'It is he!' exclaims Ahn Yune,
and buries her face in the old junkman's gown.

On that spot the brothers built a large temple,
which stands till this day, and is called the 'Niang
Niang Miao,'—'The Lady's Temple.'

Ahn Yune never left the old junkman. She became
his daughter-in-law, though her betrothed lay in the
little cemetery. She did all she could to help those who
lost their kindred in the treacherous sea. To the last
she tended the old junkman, who had many stories of
the southern seas to tell her and her mother, who often
said to her, 'It was well you saved the two richest junks.'

Such is the legend, as told by the peasant people
who now dwell in the hilly country round Ai-Shan.

It is the custom, in the long winter nights, for
friends to assemble in each other's houses; and, while
seated on their hot brick beds, to relate legend after
legend, and to repeat tale after tale. When the tales
and legends are ended, the younger people amuse themselves with riddles and conundrums, some of which are
quite ingenious.

Scholars will discover in the above story the legend of the Goddess of Mercy; and they will also see how the Buddhists here, as elsewhere, localise their myths, and so impart a vividness and verisimilitude to their marvellous narrations.

CHAPTER III.

Rugged roads—Charming scenery—A wasteful watercourse—Lotus
ponds—Arrowroot produced from lotus—The village of Wun
Shih Tang—The inn and its garnishings—Hot mineral baths—
An amusing incident.

OVER hills we jogged, and over rough and uneven
ground we jolted. The scenery was enjoyable, with
always the grand, lofty Ai-Shan in the foreground.
Sometimes it was seen against the bright blue of the
sky. Sometimes the plantations of young willows,
with their slender stems and leafless boughs, formed a
fairy screen to veil the mountain.

After about twenty miles of this road we suddenly
descended into the almost dry bed of a mountain torrent.
Acres and acres of land, swept over by the stream when
in flood, were now dry sand, which the least breath of
wind sent blowing about in clouds.

On the borders of this stream is a large tract of
land where the lotus is grown in hot-water ponds. The
water is so hot that during winter it does not freeze.
This lotus is a water-lily. The root is ground into
farina, and makes a very good kind of arrowroot, used
by the natives. Lotus-growing is a large branch of
industry, as this farina is in great demand, and is sold
at four hundred cash per catty—that is, about two
shillings per pound weight.

Passing the lotus ponds, we came to the village of Wun Shih Tang. In the east end of it is a building resembling a temple. In large Chinese characters, the public are informed that on the east side of this building there is a bath for men, on the west side one for women.

We stopped at an inn near the baths, and were ushered into a large room entirely destitute of furniture, save a small, narrow table and a bench to match. Neither would keep steady, partly on account of the irregularities of the mud floor, and partly because the carpenter (for the sake of variety, probably) had been careful that not two of the legs should be of the same length. We hunted up stones of various thicknesses, and, to ensure a level surface for our teacups, we propped up the feet of the table. This process has to be gone through at almost every inn.

After a hurried luncheon in the presence of a great number of spectators, we had a talk with the people who came to greet us. Some of them were members of the church. All of them were more or less acquainted with the truths of the Christian religion. As they had fallen into a state of religious lukewarmness, they were warned of their danger and exhorted as to their duty.

The Christians in the village were pleasant, and looked so much tidier and so much more intelligent than their neighbours, that I rejoiced.

With one of the Christian women for a guide, I visited the bath for women. We entered a gate, passed through a little labyrinth, and reached the large square room where the bath was. The bathing tank was faced round with stone on three sides; on the fourth there was some movable contrivance for an outlet to the water. There were steps running all round the tank. The topmost ledge was piled with garments of all descriptions. The bath was almost full of women and girls—the owners of the garments.

The girls were enjoying the bath in a most boisterous fashion, splashing evidently to their own satisfaction, but to the annoyance of the women ; for, as I entered, I heard a most resounding slap administered, and an accompanying threat to drown the delinquent if she did not keep quiet. Neither the slapping nor the threat had so much effect in producing quiet as the entrance of a foreign lady.

It was not an intrusion, however, as they were all pleased to see me. Several of the bathers were old friends, and immediately began a most animated conversation, chiefly in the style of the catechism, 'How had I come?' 'How long was I going to stay?' 'Had I had a good journey?' 'Would I have a bath?' They were kind enough to offer all to get out, run the bath off, and let it fill afresh. I thanked them, but `declined. The water must have been very hot, as some of them looked as red as the proverbial lobster.

An idea got suddenly into the heads of the girls that they would lose the fun of my starting if they did not immediately dress. So four or five of the wildest little lasses got out of the bath, and dragged their garments from amongst the piles on the edge of the tank. Suddenly something was projected into the middle, and went down with a splash. I thought a dog had espied his mistress and leaped in. However, a young and pretty woman screamed out, and in an instant dived after the submerged something, and fished up a baby ! With all haste she cleared its mouth and eyes from the water, and seating herself on the step, half under water, proceeded to comfort the poor little thing. It proved to be a baby three months old, who had been laid on a small quilt. A big girl roughly pulled the quilt, hunting for her jacket, and thus sent the child spinning into the water.

The little mite did not seem the worse for his ducking ; and, as his wardrobe consisted of a jacket and a cap, there was not much harm done. The cap was missing. A neighbour felt about the tank with her feet, and soon brought up the scarlet head-dress. I don't know how the baby liked the dip, but it caused great mirth to the crowd of girls round the bath. Order was restored, and the girls proceeded to make their toilettes, amid a good deal of scolding and much laughter. The real offender made off with only a portion of her wardrobe in her hand, and nothing on but her shoes.

I went to visit at the houses of our church-members, and was pleased to see the neatness and cleanliness of their apartments. One woman proudly showed me how she had set aside the time-honoured custom of having the cooking-stoves, or rather coppers, placed at the sides of the doorway. She had them put at one end of the house-place. ' So,' she said, ' you can pass in and out without soiling your skirts or blowing the ashes about.' Her daughter, a young bride, was busy preparing her trousseau. That morning a friend had presented her with an ordinary chair—a luxury they did not before possess, the sitting accommodation being generally limited to a narrow bench—simply a perch, not a seat. A countryman usually, in lieu of a seat, sits literally on his heels.

We made several visits, and it was pleasant to find

a great amount of comfort and happiness amongst the people. The village street has been recently paved. Outside the bath-house there were two wells faced with stone. The villagers come to these for hot water for domestic purposes. As we passed, two children and an old woman were busily washing turnips at the wells. This water must be a great boon to the villagers.

These springs are constantly resorted to for health. At a certain season of the year the village is full of invalids. Rheumatic people especially are much benefited by this hot bathing. Sulphur springs are found in many parts of Shan-tung. At this place, and at Ai-Shan-Tang, the water as it comes from the spring is too hot for bathing. At another place about sixty miles off there is a spring so hot that eggs and fish can be cooked in it. The name of that spring is Chau Yuen. On the Shan-tung promontory, at a place called Wun-tung Hien, there are seven or eight hot sulphur springs, and near that place there are numerous caves and grottoes.

CHAPTER IV.

LEAVING Wun Shih Tang, a short time brought us to
the Old Highway we had left two days before. It is
always much pleasanter to travel on the main roads
than in the country lanes, which, though pretty, are
very rough. In a mountainous district the fatigue of
getting over them in a shendzle is rather trying. This
evening we were fortunate enough to get into a comfortable inn just in time to secure the only apartment in
it fit for a lady. We had scarcely taken possession when
eight or ten travellers arrived—young Chinese gentlemen, who looked rather disappointed when they found
there was no better accommodation for them than the
common room, where their companions might not be
so scrupulously clean as they would desire. However,
they took their disappointment philosophically, particularly as they knew that possession was, at a Chinese
inn, the whole ten points of the law. In an incredibly
short time every corner of the inn-yard was full of carts,

mules with pack-saddles loaded, and donkeys with immense panniers.

Next morning we passed through Whang Hien, a large and very busy city, which has always been considered unfriendly to foreigners. Its citizens have the reputation of not being at all particular on points of etiquette, of being rough in manners, but always successful as merchants. They have a slight peculiarity of speech which shows that they are natives. Sometimes a Whang Hien man will be greatly amused if you tell him you know by his tone he has come from that city. There is a great deal of wealth in Whang Hien, but no special manufacture; it is merely a great caravanserai. The city has a fine wall; the gates are in good preservation. The main street is, perhaps, the busiest place I have seen during this journey.

In the evening we came to a quiet little place called Pe Ma, or White Horse Town. It got its name from a Taoist legend of a white horse, as visionary as the Flying Dutchman. The horse was possessed by one of the eight immortals. It carried the owner thousands of miles in a day, and when he halted he hid it away in his wallet. He is one of those who are supposed to have entered immortality without suffering bodily dissolution.

We had quite a long talk with the women, who had often seen foreign gentlemen, but not ladies. The landlord made a journey into the country, to bring a favourite grand-daughter to see the foreign lady. She was a merry, bonny little maiden, dressed in all the colours of the rainbow, and almost as harmoniously blended. She was made perfectly happy by the gift of a pictorial magazine and some pieces of foreign cloth.

A bit of black velveteen rejoiced her immensely. 'Oh! what splendid tips for my brother's shoes that will make!' she exclaimed. She was a loving, joyous little child.

We passed the lively town of Whang San Kwan, which was busy, a market having been held that morning. In the afternoon we saw a great many peasants returning from the fair. They had a pleasing look of contentment. Not one of them seemed to have indulged in drinking anything stronger than tea. Almost every man among them was carrying some article for household use. They had brooms, hay-forks, pot-lids, sheets of matting, baskets, wooden buckets, straw sandals, teapots, toys for children, and a variety of other domestic utensils. These peasants depend on their little markets for the necessary supplies. In many villages there is not a single shop. All over the country there are pedlars selling oil, cloth, and the various little silk trimmings and silk thread so necessary to beautify the tiny shoes of which every Chinese woman is so proud. These pedlars are complete plunderers. They charge exorbitantly. Unless a Chinese woman is quick-witted, they will, in the most glaring way, add up the items wrongly, but always putting the error on the side that fills their own pockets.

The country we passed through was not very interesting. We crossed a great many watercourses, almost dry at this time, but in the rainy season what sweeping torrents they must be! I was quite distressed at the amount of land covered by these mountain torrents. They spread out over acres and acres of ground strewn with sand and loose stones. The inhabitants make use of them as drying-grounds for their vermicelli.

When I saw the poles, and long white hanks drying,
I thought we had come on a Chinese bleaching establishment. The finest, snowy white, was hanging on poles
in immense skeins, just as yarn is when in process of
drying. Vermicelli, made from a very glutinous bean,
is a great article of export to Hong Kong, Singapore,
and the South of China. The natives rarely use it
except at the new year. They count it too precious
to be wasted in home consumption.

Lying between these large tracts of waste land are
fine fertile fields, most carefully cultivated. Wheat is
just now looking its richest green. By-and-by, many
varieties of Indian corn, several kinds of millet,
panicum, and buckwheat, beans, peas, turnips, carrots,
endless varieties of melons, from the gigantic water-
melon to the fine-flavoured musk-melon, not much
larger than an orange, egg plants, enormous vegetable
marrows, cucumbers, and smaller vegetables of all kinds,
will be found in great abundance in this plain. Here
and there are small patches of upland rice, which grows
like wheat, and needs no irrigation. Indigo, saffron,
madder, and many other dye-stuffs grow on the farms ;
also tobacco and the cotton plant. They have sweet
sorghum,[1] from which they make a kind of thin syrup.
On the hills they have a plant from which they make
coarse, bitter tea, and on their own lands, by the sides
of streams, they can raise timber enough for building
purposes. Altogether, they are fairly independent of
the outer world. The only time of distress among them
is when the fruits of the earth fail.

In little sheltered valleys we come on orchards. The
blossoms are just opening on the cherry trees. In a few

[1] A species of Barbadoes millet.

days these orchards will be ablaze in the pink glories of the peach and the soft white of the pear.

The villages look comfortable; most of the houses are built of stone, and roofed with blue tiles. The village street has invariably its idol shrine, and generally a pond, lively with ducks and geese. The outside yards are usually carefully swept. Inside the houses is a sort of organised untidiness, for the houses are shop and house in one, where they grind the corn for their daily need, spin the cotton, weave it into cloth, and often prepare their dye-stuffs.

The peasant life here at present is something like the life that Scottish farm-labourers and peasants lived in the time of the poet Burns and the days of Sir Walter Scott. Amid all this agricultural population I am sure there are many who, although they do not sing of the

' Wee, modest, crimson-tippit flower,'

yet praise some Chinese gem with equal fervour. I have come across not a few of poetic taste and alive to the beauties of nature.

CHAPTER V.

Arrival at the city of Laichow-foo—Our experiences there—Boys :
their pranks, and their defeat—The traffic as seen in the inn-
yard—Trip through the city—Steatite slabs, cups, and ornaments—Fine marble quarries—Contrast between cities and
villages—Our departure ; a block on the road—Chats with the
natives and wayfarers—A bridge out of the way—A beautiful
archway.

A few hours' ride next morning brought us to the city
of Laichow-foo. My husband immediately went into
the city with books, and left me at the inn, to give
attention to matters relating to provender. Crowds of
boys came rushing in to stare at the foreign woman.
I was speedily considered fair prey by a small army
of young ruffians. To escape from them, I closed the
double-leaved door, and retired to a corner with my
books. They crept quietly up to the door, and suddenly,
with a bang, opened both sides of it, and whooped and
howled distractingly. Outside there was quite an embankment of faces. Again I shut the door and bolted
it, and hoped for quietness, but the hooting and noise
of the boys continued. They shouted, ' Devil woman,
open the door ! ' Then they began to use language which
they would not have used had they known that I
understood it. This was not to be borne ; I opened the
door to make friends with these boys. That crowd of
youngsters had something like half-a-dozen Chinese

'Tom Sawyers,' hooting and yelling as if possessed. Out I came, and said, 'Look here, boys. Have you got fathers ?'

'Yes! yes! yes!' all over the crowd.

'Have you got mothers ?'

'Yes! yes! yes!' more loudly.

The ringleader pointed to a meek-looking little lad. 'His mother is dead; will *you* take him?' This of course raised a laugh.

'Have devils fathers and mothers ?'

'No! no! no!' very loudly.

'Well, boys, I cannot be one; for I have a father and a mother—an old mother of eighty, far, far away over the sea, in America.'

The boys looked disconcerted. The crowd began to melt away. There was no more fun to be got by worrying a woman who talked to them like this. I told them of their Father in heaven, and of all His goodness to them, and of His Son, our Saviour. 'That is a Jesus-religion woman,' said a man on the edge of the crowd. The boys retired discomfited, but not convinced; for the ringleader put his head round the angle of a building, and, as a parting salute, shouted, 'Kwei Tzl Lao poh,' *alias* 'Devil woman.' However, I was left in profound peace till my husband returned, after having traversed the city and sold many of his books.

In this inn-yard of Laichow-foo I counted forty-five animals at one time. There were carts, large and small, laden with goods of all kinds. Some were going west with bales of piece-goods, Manchester cottons, and woollen cloths. Some were *en route* for Chefoo, with native produce, straw braid, for England and America, vermicelli, for the South of China, great quantities of medicinal drugs, barks, roots, and dye-stuffs, the saffron thistle, and indigo, besides miscellaneous articles for home consumption.

In the neighbourhood of Laichow-foo there is some fine and very beautiful steatite, of a soft grey colour. As the steatite is chiefly found in laminæ, it is only used for ornamental work. Broad slabs of it, finely grained, are thought very handsome. These are mounted on stands of wood, and placed in libraries.

It is pleasant to visit the shops and observe the variety of articles for use and ornament devised by the ingenuity of the people. The largest were trays made of slabs of steatite with borders of carved wood. There were teacups, little teapots, saucers, carved gods innumerable, and all sorts of grotesque figures of the same material. There were also some basins of solid stone cut out in compartments. The most artistic thing I saw was a piece of steatite of a soft grey colour grained with white and black, and carved out in the form of a lotus leaf with its edges curled up, so as to make a large flat cup. There was a great variety of screens, on which the steatite had been carefully carved to represent fruit and flowers; and, as the flowers were tinted, the whole effect was pleasing.

In this neighbourhood there are immense marble quarries. The marble is quarried out in very large slabs, and is used extensively for gravestones. It is very white and durable. The longer it is exposed to the weather the whiter it looks.

We left the city of Laichow-foo, with its handsome walls and imposing gateways, with reluctance. It has a much cleaner look than most Chinese cities. The people are pleasant. They are not so busy with merchandise as to have little leisure for study. The literary men among them are fond of reading, and discussing the literary magazines. The shops are always interesting, from the great variety of stonework in them.

A walled city has always a handsome look that straggling places lack. The defined wall hides many deformities. Some towns lose themselves in the country, or the country gets swallowed up in the town. In such cases there is a want of decision, as if neither town nor country had strength of mind enough to say, ' I'll stop here.' The moat surrounding a walled city often improves its appearance, filled, as it sometimes is, with the pink water-lily and other aquatic plants, while the green banks are starry with wild flowers and shady and cool with waving willows that grow most luxuriantly.

We were brought to a halt just outside of a small town a little beyond Laichow-foo. We found a large cart, laden with bales of cotton and vermicelli, blocking up the entire gateway. One of the mules drawing the cart had slipped on the smooth stones of the incline at the gateway and fallen. Our muleteers, powerful men; helped to release the fallen mule and to remove the block from the gateway.

While our party waited for the clearing of the way, we had a talk with the people. One rather nice-looking man begged very eagerly for medicine to cure his eyes. He said that he was a block-cutter, that his eyes had become sore, and that now he was quite unable to do any work at engraving, and so his family was suffering. We advised him to go to Chefoo, that he might be healed. He said that he would be only too glad to go, if he could be restored to fitness for working. Over the

GATEWAY OF A WALLED VILLAGE.

(*From a Chinese Engraving.*)

gateway where the cart was stuck fast was a motto cut in the stone,

'KINGDOM PEACEFUL—FAMILY HAPPY.'

We are frequently crossing bridges that span the dry earth, while the water wanders off at its own sweet will, and looks back, as if enquiring of the empty arch, 'Don't you wish you could catch me?' Just after passing one of these empty bridges we came on a very fine old willow tree, growing by the side of the vagrant water. In some bygone storm it had been partially uprooted, and now it made a complete span of the road, rising in a fine arch. From the centre of the arch there had grown up, as if planted in the old trunk, four fine trees. It was a natural curiosity, and made quite a pretty object, seen far off on the highway.

CHAPTER VI.

The town of Sa Hoh—The centre of the great straw-braid district—
The producers : their diligence and expertness—A Chinese
funeral—Preparations made at night, and the reason why—A
description of the rites, procession, and obsequies.

TWENTY miles west from Laichow-foo we reached Sa Hoh,
the centre of the district in which so much straw braid
or plait is made. It is prepared from wheat straw. The
natives are very expert at plaiting it. At every door
stood girls and women busily plaiting, their fingers
going as nimbly over the braid as though there was no
toil in forming those wondrous bunches of fine straw
plait. The finest of it is plaited by women from seventeen to thirty years of age. When older than thirty-
five expertness fails them, and, as a rule, they do not
plait so well. This plaiting is one of the most important industries of Shan-tung. Great quantities of
the plait are exported to New York and to England.
It is also dyed in very fine colours. The mixed braids
of green and white, and of magenta and white, are
exceedingly pretty.

The town has improved immensely since I saw it
first in 1873. Many new and handsome places of
business have been opened. Many houses have recently
been built. There is a general well-to-do look about
the people. Certainly foreign trade has done a great

deal, not only for Sa Hoh, but for all the surrounding district.

The whole town was astir because of a very important funeral. A funeral is always a cause of excitement among the Chinese. They have a great appetite for the pleasure to be got from a large burial. The liveliest music is then played, and, if the people have money, there is a good deal of feasting.

We were disturbed the whole night by the firing of crackers, the promenading of the orchestra, and the clattering of their cymbals and other instruments. The age of the man to be buried is announced at certain stages in the orchestral performance by the firing of guns. This poor man was seventy-eight; so we had quite a night of firing and broken slumbers. I asked the people why they made all this parade in the night. They said, ' In the daytime we are too busy with straw braid to pay attention to buryings.'

Just at dawn the procession was formed, and the old man was carried to his long home in a little yew-shaded graveyard outside the town. His age having been told by firing, his history was shadowed forth in the order of the funeral procession. The following is the order of procession :—

Two rough fellows dragging the effigies of two public lictors, not toys but life size.

A man carrying a supply of fire-crackers.

Two men with red flags—the banners of the house.

Two men dragging effigies of lions.

Two men waving large placards, with a character on them which signifies to all people that henceforth all personal matters with this man are at an end, and no personal quarrels, &c., are to continue in his family.

D

Four shrines, with offerings for the gods. The offerings include flowers, fruits, meats, and wine.

Four paper houses, with dresses, furniture, and servants all complete. These four houses signify that the man has four sons, who each provide him with a house for the world of shades. If the sons are dead their descendants attend to this.

An effigy of his private horse, riderless.

An effigy of his wife's mule, with her seated on it.

An effigy of his private cart. These have all their suitable attendants, life size.

A number of mourners in the second degree, their blue clothes showing under the white.

All the schoolboys of the family.

A few friends, literary graduates, in their best robes.

A few more special mourners of the second degree.

Two effigies of the gate-keepers of hell. These are carried about by men *inside* of them, and are made immensely large. They are represented as carrying heavy brass maces. All this is to insure that no one comes out of hell to drag the man into it.

A handsome gilt shrine with crimson canopy, carried by four bearers, containing offerings for the dead, bread, meat, fish, pork, and usually a boar's head.

A man carrying fire-crackers.

Priests, who are also musicians, and discourse music all the way to the tomb. When they stop playing crackers are fired off.

The tablet of the village or district god.

Men bearing flying banners of strips of silk. These are to catch any evil influences that are in the air, and that might harm the dead.

The empty sedan-chair of deceased, with trumpeters following.

The chief mourners.

Man with bowl.

The hearse, borne by sixteen bearers, with paper attendants inside.

The coffin on a bier.

The chief mourners (women), who remain kneeling and wailing till the crackers are fired, telling that the coffin has left the village.

Several masters of ceremonies form the procession into proper order. As the coffin is brought out all the chief mourners kneel in front of the hearse, the eldest male relative holding in his hands a very large bowl. This bowl contains the ashes of all the dead man's private letters, and all personal things that he has not put in the hands of his secretary. Immediately after the man dies these are burned, and the ashes are put into a large handsome bowl prepared for the purpose. Just as the coffin is put into the hearse this bowl is broken to atoms by the man who holds it, and who utters some words, signifying that the dead man has done with all things here. At the same time an attendant woman cuts through a double scarlet cord, and says, 'The cord is loosed.' This is done only if his wife survives him. This has a most solemn effect, especially as all have been silent till now. But now the floodgates of sorrow are opened, and the women wail in most heartrending tones.

'The loosing of the cord' has reference to a very ancient phrase that is always used when betrothals are spoken of. The phrase runs in Chinese, 'Their feet have been tied together.' How similar to the words in the Book of Ecclesiastes, 'the bowl broken,' 'the cord loosed'! Shan-tung is classic China, and here are found

the oldest religious traditions.   I have given the order
of this procession.   In large cities the funerals are much
more imposing.

The wheat straw of Sa Hoh is a curious instance of
the effect of soil on plants, showing that the virtue does
not always lie in the plant, but in soil and environment.
With a view to bring the straw braid nearer to the port
of shipment, several farmers sowed the seed from Sa
Hoh in the immediate vicinity of Chefoo.   It produced
most excellent wheat, but the straw was worthless for
plaiting.

CHAPTER VII.

A genuine country fair—The buyers and sellers : their commodities, ways, and keenness—Barter—Domestic cotton spinning : its utility and importance—The town of Han Ting—A touching sight at the inn—The city of Wei Hien; how it was taken—The inn-yard.

NEXT morning we came to a small town where a genuine country fair was going on. I was astonished to see so many women buying and selling. There were charred and wrinkled forms of womankind, also middle-aged peasant women, and a small proportion of young women. At these fairs one can read the life of the people.

At the entrance to the town is a lovely little temple built on a height. The temple is like a miniature palace, and is surrounded by very handsome yew and *arbor vitæ* trees all around. It has the look of a toy palace for some fairy princess from Liliput Land. In the square in front of this temple a noisy market was being held, a genuine small country fair.

The flight of steps which led up to the idol shrine had been taken possession of by the women. On the lowest step sat a rather pretty woman about twenty-four years of age, displaying for sale a fine black fowl. I would fain have stopped and bought it, as our stock of provisions was low, and we had not been able to get fowls in some places through which we lately passed; but I thought she would have asked six times too much for it. Higher up the steps leading to the shrine eggs were placed in baskets of all sizes, and salted eggs in great abundance, carefully guarded by old crones. Hot steamed bread was carried about in baskets exactly like our straw beehives, with the movable tops for lids. An active-looking young rustic had skilfully piled up a pyramid of leeks. Next to the leeks was a butcher's stall, where various sections of good pork were hanging. The pork-butcher was hard to bargain with. A spruce young husband was trying to barter a string of yarn cops of his wife's spinning for one of the finest pieces of pork chops. As our shendzles stopped, the young man said, ' You won't often see such fine spinning ! '

' Who spun it ? ' said the butcher.

' My people at home.'

' I don't want fine thread. We are not weaving cloth this year.'

' I'll give you the half of them for these ribs of pork,' persisted the husband.

Our shendzles passed on. I suppose the man had the pork after all. There seemed to be little money passing in the market. Most of the business was done by barter. It takes a long time to dispose of things in that way. It may be a primitive mode of business, but I could see it was very inconvenient. An old woman with a basket of cotton, snowy white, just as it comes from the pod, wants three very large Shan-tung cabbages. The vendor offers two. She insists on having three. She puts a handful or two of the cotton into her lap, and offers again. The bargain is concluded;

she gets two cabbages for the cotton *minus* the two handfuls. At one end of the street there is a regular barter of spun yarn for raw cotton.

In the poor peasant households each daughter-in-law on her arrival is presented by her mother-in-law with a pound of cotton. Sometimes she is presented with two pounds of cotton. With this she is expected to clothe her husband and herself; and it depends on her industry whether they shall be comfortably clad or in rags. She spins the cotton. Her husband takes it to the fair. For one pound of very finely spun yarn the merchant will give two pounds of carded cotton. If it be indifferently spun he may give only a pound and a half. If she gets two pounds of cotton, at her next spinning she retains one pound. The husband again takes the other and barters it for two. It is astonishing how much yarn an active young woman who is an expert spinner will thus accumulate during a year. In the winter months it is quite cheery to hear the swish of the shuttle and the click-clack of the treadles as the men make the yarn into cloth, for weaving is always done by men, such work being thought too heavy for women.

A yarn merchant makes quite a profit. He sells the yarn either to professional weavers or to families whose spinning has been deficient. Native cloth is worth much more than that from Manchester looms, and it wears twice as long. City people do not spin so much. If the *Via Victoria*[1] brings in its wake spinning-jennies and sewing-machines, what will China's daughters do? No hum of spinning-wheel, no elaborate stitching! Are England's daughters happier with

---

[1] *Via Victoria*, as the railway has been aptly called—true both of its era and its issue.

Cambridge examinations and art galleries than were our great-grandmothers with their spinning-wheels ? I leave the West to answer this.

But we have not seen all the fair. It begins at the temple and wanders all up the village street. The cake-sellers and sweetmeat-sellers get cash. Of course the toffee is as attractive to young China as to our home children. The sweetmeat-seller drops his cash into a long piece of bamboo, which makes a capital purse, and the children stand round and watch for the drop of the coins, so that they may hear the rattling noise.

From Sah Hoh to Wei Hien the country is very lovely, though flat, but on every side are the spreading wheat fields. In consequence of the value of the straw braid for export, as much wheat is sown as possible. We stopped at Han Ting, a few miles from Wei Hien, and had long talks with the people, who remembered much of the former teachings. The inn-yard was not so crowded as usual. I was interested in little twin children, of whom their father, quite a young man, was exceedingly proud. As the mules were prancing hither and thither, he got anxious about his little ones, and, for safety, sat them in a manger. These Eastern mangers are large troughs, standing on four feet, and are movable. We thought of the Babe of Bethlehem and the manger cradle.

All along the outside of the town the rope-makers were busy making splendid ropes. The flax or hemp used by them was of a fine colour and very long in the fibre. Their winding machines were most ingenious, and were worked most efficiently. Some of the ropes were immensely thick and hard-twined. The large coils of them must have been very valuable.

In this neighbourhood the handsome barn-door fowls, something like our Dorkings, constantly attracted my attention.

The next stage on our journey was the city of Wei Hien, which lies in the centre of an immense plain, which, in the autumn, is like a great ocean of waving grain. It is a most important place—a busy, wealthy city, surrounded by a fine, lofty, crenelated wall, with only here and there an embrasure. The inhabitants have the reputation of being proud, turbulent, and very exclusive. After the treaty of 1860 they resolved that, although the government had allowed barbarians to travel throughout China, their city at least would not open its gates to them. After some years a foreigner presented himself at the gates. Great was the consternation. The whole city was moved. The elders assembled. ' Tell him he can't come in.'

' He says he is coming in.'

' Call out the military, and let them defend the gate.'

' He says the soldiers belong to the Emperor, and he carries the Emperor's order to go all over Shan-tung, and he is coming into Wei Hien, as this is part of Shan-tung.'

' Fix spears, and defend the gate.'

' So it shall be.'

But the foreigner is quietly walking through the gate and up the main street. The soldiers, with spears fixed, and eyes fixed too, gaze at the tall bearded foreigner walking alone with the imperial passport open in his hand. What could they do ?

So Wei Hien received the much-dreaded barbarian; and ever since, the city has not only been open but kindly to foreigners.

The foreigner who first walked into the city has again and again visited it, has established a station in it, and now has arrived on another visit.

It was early afternoon, and Dr. Williamson almost immediately went into the city, taking with him many Scriptures and books. I remained in the inn. Soon old friends came with kindly welcome and kindly questions : ' Had I brought my daughter ? ' ' Would I stay a long time ? ' After a while an old friend who had got much teaching in the doctrines of religion came. His greeting was warm and earnest. He spoke of our hospital at Chefoo, and said, ' You should make one in Wei Hien ; every one would like it. Wei Hien people all like foreigners. Even the mandarins say foreigners come to teach people to be wise and good.' This man and all his household have embraced Christianity.

Many women and girls came to see me. On former occasions I had lived in the north-western suburbs, but now many of these women had come all across that great city to see me again. It was pleasant to be recognised by them, and to find they had not forgotten what I had attempted to teach them.

CHAPTER VIII.

Chinese ladies—A Chinese lady's dinner—Its cuisine, etiquette,
and elegance.

I HAD formerly visited Wei Hien, and had many kind
friends within its walls. So, some time after our
arrival, I sent in my card to one of their houses, in the
evening. One of the servants came to me with a return
card, and a message from the ladies asking me to excuse
them from receiving me, because they were out of
health, and their house was not in complete order, and
saying that they would be glad if I would visit them on
the following day. Early next morning a fine cart
drawn by a handsome mule came rattling into the
courtyard of the inn. In the cart, as escort, was the
personal maid of the Chinese lady at the head of the
house. This maid was a shrewd, sensible woman of
forty-five. She said that, lest I might not like the
jolting of the cart, the lady had sent her sedan-chair
for me, and a lictor to clear the way. Which would I
have, the cart or the chair? I preferred the cart.
From the front of the cart the lictor brought a stool,
placed it firmly against the wheel, and so I mounted a
conveyance which, in China, takes the place of a private
carriage. The maid sat behind, because the front seat
is the best. The curtain, in the centre of which was a
square of glass, was let down, and off we rattled, the

coachman holding the reins and running alongside,
this being the dignified thing to do. What a bumping
and knocking about from side to side over the rough
stones! Still, it was pleasant to look at the shops, and
watch the concourse of people. The crowds on the
street were most polite; for, was not this foreigner
seated in the family chariot of the proud possessor of
the highest poles in the city? In China it is not the
man with the deepest purse who is entitled to honour,
but the man who, for some special merit and good
conduct, is entitled to put up at his front gate the tallest
poles—red lacquered poles, like giant masts.

After driving for half-an-hour we reached the house,
close to the city wall, within the east gate. There
stood the poles, one on each side of the entrance to the
mansion, and kept in their places by four enormous
blocks of granite. These poles, a greatly desired mark
of distinction, were about sixty feet high, with ornamental cross-trees, and varnished with imperial vermilion. As the cart drew up at the door a great crowd
collected. It was quite orderly, and made a line for me
to pass through the gateway and into the inner court.
Here the lictor stopped the crowd, and ordered the
door to be closed. The maid apologised to me for not
reaching the ladies' apartments through the grand
library, because, since the death of the master of the
house, his widow had locked it up, as it contained many
very valuable objects of art, which she feared might be
stolen. In this library was the coffin of an uncle
waiting for interment for twenty-one years, because
that branch of the family were not able to afford a
handsome funeral.

We passed into a court behind the library, and

from thence into the ladies' court. Close to the great
door of the ladies' court, as it was opened, stood the
eldest lady of the family. She stood alone in the centre.
On each side of her, drawn up in lines, were the other
ladies of the household. On her left were the sons'
wives, their children and attendants. On her right
were her married daughter and other female members

A CHINESE LADY.

of the family, with their attendants. It was quite an
imposing sight. I am sure there were over fifty women
in that courtyard. We saluted each other by clasping
one hand over the other and making a salaam. Then
the old lady, with words of kindly welcome, took my
hand and led me up to the top of the stone steps, the
ladies following in two lines, first left, then right. We
saluted each other formally. Then the lines were

broken up, and we had such a greeting of old friends.
The eldest son's wife, a pretty woman of forty, claimed
me as her friend. The eldest daughter, a woman of
forty-five, also claimed me. They hugged and patted
and petted me in a most un-Chinese fashion. They
were most unfeignedly delighted to see me, and exclaimed, ' Why have you been so long of coming ? '

They told me their sorrows ;—how the head of the
house had died ; how the eldest grandson had died ;
how the two younger daughters of the house had died ;
and how, when one after another died, they always
wanted me to comfort them. Then they told me that
the second son was very ill, and could not live long.
' Would you mind sitting in his room and talking to
him ? We promised him you would.' I said I would
be only too pleased to go. We went into the Tai Tai's
room. One half of it was screened off by a silken damask
curtain, a perfect piece of beauty, gold ground with
crimson flowers, and broad stripes of pale sea-green.
In front of the curtain was a low ottoman, covered with
fine crimson felt, and in the centre of the ottoman a
handsome brazier of brass filigree work was placed, in
which charcoal was burning. I was taken to a seat on the
ottoman, and asked to warm my fingers. Then a silver
pipe was presented—a water pipe, in which the smoke
is purified by passing through water. I declined to
smoke. Then tea in beautiful cups with silver saucers
was offered. The saucers were not round but oval,
pointed at either end. Various kinds of sweetmeats
were given with the tea, the finest being crystallised
Siberian crabs. These were most delicious. The ladies
told me that every year they had a supply of them from
Peking.

We had a pleasant talk of the various changes in our households. We spoke of how the Da Sian Niang's daughter was married; how they would not give her to an opium-smoking husband; how my daughter was married, and when she would come to visit me.

Suddenly a movement of the damask curtain, and a voice saying 'Mamma!' in our own identical tones, startled me. Behind the curtain was a luxuriously furnished divan, and there lay the sick son. He was most handsomely dressed. As he extended his hands they looked like ivory. His face, though pale, was not unpleasant. A habitual opium smoker, he was wasting away.

He greeted me most pleasantly, talked of his old friends, and asked where they were. He mentioned particularly Dr. W. A. Henderson, who, he said, had been most kind to him and to his father. I said, 'I fear we disturb you.' He replied, 'No, I like so much to hear you all talking.' He was most affectionate to his mother and sisters, and spoke kindly to his wife. He evidently had the feelings of a true gentleman. We talked of Russia, and of European news that he had read in the 'Globe Magazine.' We spoke much of religious matters. He told me he was afraid to become a Christian, lest when he died he would not go to the same place as his ancestors. 'All the New Testament,' he said, 'was good, but the Revelation of St. John was splendid.' Our conversation was mixed with talks of railways, the falling of the Tay bridge, and current news.

After a time we adjourned to the apartments of the younger ladies, and had luncheon of confections, fruit, pastry, salad, and tea. Only the old Tai Tai ate with me. The young wives and daughters ate afterwards.

The divan on which we sat, and on which was placed the small dining-table, was covered with a magnificent wadded quilt. The centre piece was yellow silk with crimson brocade pattern, richly mixed with gold. I think these gorgeous damasks must be like the cloth of beaten gold spoken of in Scripture. The opposite divan was covered with a quilt of greater beauty—white satin embroidered in pink and gold and green. The border was a wide piece of pale sea-green satin. I never saw such costly damasks. Perhaps the ladies had beautified their rooms with spoils from the old mandarin's hoard. They told me that these damasks and the elaborate embroidery that hung as a drapery on the front of the *kangs* were a present. A rich man in China often fears to show his wealth, as he is so apt to be victimised by the officials. While we were at luncheon the whole household of women came in and partook of melon seeds and sweetmeats. Some of the nieces of the old Tai Tai came in with their children. There were many very fine-looking women amongst them. They all talked gently and pleasantly.

I spoke to them for a long time on the truths of our religion. They were attentive listeners, and asked a number of most intelligent questions. Two or three of them whispered together for a short time, and then the eldest daughter said, ' We have one important thing we wish to know. We are always thinking of it and talking of it. Many of our family are dead, and this brother will soon die. This is the important question : Where do people go when they die ? Do men and women go to the same place ? '

I told them of the city that hath no need of the sun, of the pearly gates, and of the golden streets, of the inhabitants of the city who hunger no more, neither thirst any more. I told them of the multitude which no man can number, of all nations and kindreds and people and tongues, and 'of God the Judge of all, and of the spirits of *just men made perfect.'*

The great event of the day was dinner. I had hoped to return to our inn before evening, but as I found they would be disappointed if I did not stay to dinner, I reluctantly consented.

Just at sunset dinner was served. None but the old Tai Tai and I dined, although there was ample provision for the thirty or forty women and girls who sat round about the room, talking and amusing the little ones. The table, about a foot high, was laid again on the cloth of gold divan. The eldest son's wife sat by the side of the old Tai Tai to assist her. The eldest daughter of the house sat by my side, to give me what help I needed in selecting the most *recherché* viands. Various women servants waited table. A relative—an aunt, I think—whose duty it is, began the dinner by pouring from an exquisite little china teapot some very toothsome sauce into a porcelain spoon that was laid on a saucer for each. Another relative brought wine in two silver measures. The eldest daughter-in-law brought in wheaten cakes as thin as paper. The eldest daughter brought in two napkins, called food arresters. These were beautiful squares of silk about the size of a large dinner napkin. The one handed to me was of pale olive-green, printed in colours, pink roses being the chief patterns. It had a lining of pale pink satin; one corner of it was folded down, and a silk cord sewn on to serve as a button latch. The lady deftly fastened this on the topmost button of my dress, laid the corner

E

straight down the front of my dress, and spread the
other two corners out towards my elbows. The old Tai
Tai was similarly adorned. The prevailing colour of her
napkin was blue. The lining of it was of gold colour.
Ladies strive to have these napkins in as much variety
as possible.

After we were arrayed in the napkins dinner was
served. The viands were deliciously cooked, and as course
after course was sent in I became quite bewildered.
There were fowl, fish, pork, salad, eggs, savory stews
of all things mentionable and unmentionable, *bêche de
mer*, steaming hot bread of the whitest, chips of ham
of the finest flavour, confections exquisite in taste and
appearance, and, last of all, a tiny basin of soup, with a
slightly acid flavour and a mucilaginous consistence.
This wound up a dinner fit for an empress. If refine-
ment is seen in the manner in which we prepare and
serve our food, then the Chinese are a refined people.
The decorations on the various dishes were highly
artistic. When dinner was ended, two beautifully lacquered basins were brought in, with hot water and
a small napkin, which the lady wrung out and handed
to me; so we did not wipe our hands on the lovely
satin pinafores. There were about forty young and
pretty women in the room. Now and then the old
Tai Tai fed some little prattlers with titbits, the little
rosebud mouths opening for them like so many little
fledglings.

Opium smoking has made sad havoc in this family.
There is scarcely a healthy member in it. The sons are
all dead save one. The grandsons are puny and sickly.
One boy of eight has never had more than three teeth,
and is not likely to have more. Another child of four

has cataract in both eyes. He was all right till he was two years of age, when the cataract was observed. It is affecting to see him turn his little eyeballs, and try to look upon his mother. She is devoted to the child, and asked me eagerly if a great doctor like Dr. Henderson was coming, and if I thought he could make her child see. It was sad to hear these women talk of opium as having blighted all their lives. The heir, a fine boy of ten, is quite like his mother, and has not a trace of his father's features. The women in the family are bent on keeping him from opium. The old grandmother tells him that if he begins to take opium, she will sell everything but the house, and divide the silver amongst the ladies of the family.

I went to say good-bye to the invalid son. I asked if I could do anything for him. He inquired if I had any coffee. He said it helped him much against opium smoking. We had a large bottle of essence of coffee, and some tins of milk, which I sent to him. He also begged me to send him two tubes of vaccine lymph. In former years we had sent it. As many as six hundred babies had been vaccinated with it in one spring by his father.

I bade these friends a most affectionate adieu. I returned to the inn in the cart. The driver was a veritable Jehu, for, in the evening, when the streets were clear of traffic, and a brilliant moon was shining, he did drive furiously.

In the morning, just as we were starting from the city, the manservant came with his master's card, wishing us a happy journey, and with a present of two red boxes of sweet cakes. It is a Chinese custom on such occasions to present such cakes, which are a substitute for the stirrup cup, and a good substitute. It is a piece of affectation to pile these little red boxes in a conspicuous place among the baggage, so that all may see how popular one is. On some carts a regular pile of them was seen, ten or twelve at least.

CHAPTER IX.

A grand archway in honour of a virtuous woman—Its ornamentation—Pleasant villages—The city of Chang Loh—Lime-kilns—Novel house-building—Sunday—Native Christians—Transmission of letters—Manufacture of twine.

THE next forenoon was fine. As we left Wei Hien we looked lingeringly back to its lofty walls, and the great powder tower that stands just outside the west gate. A mile or two from the city, on the north side of the road, we saw a most gorgeous *pei-low*, quite new, and of larger proportions and finer workmanship than any we had seen. From every ornament on it, and from every point from which anything could be hung, there floated long banners of scarlet cloth. At all the corners, also, were long draperies of scarlet cloth. The breeze was just light enough to stir the banners and give the whole a jubilant look. The grounds around were newly planted with trees. Hundreds of workmen were busy putting up a fine wall to enclose several acres of ground around this handsome monument.

Who was thus honoured? we inquired; and great was our surprise to be told that it was a lady, the wife of a great man in the city. We could not hear anything more special about her than that she had been good, and very kind to the poor and to the aged. But, alas! she had no sons to hold her memory sacred. Her husband

had been a great public benefactor, and had done good
service to the city in many ways. So, with imperial
permission, the citizens erected this gigantic monument
to perpetuate the remembrance of his wife. It had been
publicly opened a few days before, and the whole road
leading to it had a gay, holiday look. A village some
two miles beyond, in which the ancestral temple of this
family stands, was also decorated with great streamers
of scarlet. What amused me most was to see every little
idol on the roofs and gateways of the temple with a
strip of scarlet cloth tied round its throat, the ends
floating in the wind. Even the little poodles that were
running about the village had scarlet strings on their
necks.

We passed through pleasant villages shaded with
trees, and lively with young voices, the cackling of
ducks, the gossip of geese, and other cheery rural
sounds. We stopped for our mid-day halt at a very
small inn in an exceedingly pretty village, the street of
which was wide and filled on each side with small inns.
Tables were ranged on the street, and numerous travellers were taking dinner in the open air.

On the outskirts of this village we saw a number of
men making beautifully smooth sun-dried bricks. They
were kneading the clay with their feet, and then press-
ing it into an oblong mould.

All their courtyards were tidily swept up, and their
fowls, exceedingly pretty, of varied colours, were well
cared for. Almost every chanticleer had a tippet of a
different colour. There were grey cocks with sheeny
green ruffs; gold-coloured, with silvery grey; white,
with golden brown tippets; and black, with mottled
white.

Passing over a mountain ridge, we came on a village of lime-kilns on the sides of a spur of a hill. It was a very busy place. The highway ran right through the village. The lime-burners looked a wild and rough set of men, who were busily loading great wheelbarrows with the lime. This village is, I am told, entirely deserted during the winter months, as it is too cold and exposed. The huts in it are built tent-fashion—a low wall, not a foot high, for a foundation; then, long millet stalks forming a sloping roof, plastered with white lime. They looked, in the distance, exactly like canvas tents.

After crossing the limestone ridge we reached the city of Chang Loh. Here we found what, for China, was a most comfortable inn, and almost clean—brighter and lighter than the usual hostelries at which we have put up. A very early start in the morning had brought us to our halting-place while the sun was yet high; so we had time to walk about, and get interested in the people.

At one place they were building a house in rather a novel way. At each of the four corners they had erected a square, solid pillar of half-burnt brick. From one of these corners to another two long planks were fixed in the form of a trough, whose width was to be the thickness of the walls. Into this trough three men and a boy were busily shovelling mud lightly mixed with straw. After shovelling in a quantity, they laid down their spades, got into the space between the planks, and stamped most vigorously on the mud. Then another filling was succeeded by another stamping, and so on, till the mud was beaten hard. The planks were then slipped up, and the process repeated till the wall was completed. This house was entirely of mud and straw; beds, cupboards, cooking pots,—all were built in with the same materials. The cupboards were millet stalks plastered over with mud. Nearly all the walls in that village were built on the trough plan. Some of the houses were plastered over with lime, and looked bright enough. I fear they would be infested by scorpions and such crawling things as are found living in mud walls. The millet stalks also, I believe, would most likely make a very earwiggy cupboard.

The workmen had levelled the earth for the floor, and the hard knockings they made were accompanied by a sing-song kind of grunt. Looking in, I saw the floor was being pounded hard by three men, working what Shakespeare calls 'the three-man beetle,' and rapidly making the floor smooth and solid. The house was roofed over with millet stalks, plastered with mud mixed with straw. When dry, the roof would get a good solid coat of lime plaster. It was astonishing that, with such scant materials and in so short a time, they could make a tolerably comfortable dwelling.

At this city, Chang Loh, we spent the Sunday. How often it happens that Sabbaths are so calm and bright, as though heaven were so near that some of its rest, and peace, and brightness had overflowed to soothe us here!

In this neighbourhood are many native Christians, poor peasant people who are struggling upward to the light. In these weak ones are the germs of the true righteousness whereby this nation will, in the future, be exalted.

This was the third point on the route from which we dispatched letters. We made them up in a large packet, and gave it to the muleteer of a cart travelling towards Chefoo. Outside the package was written that, on delivery within a specified time, the bearer would receive one hundred and fifty copper cash—about eight pence of English money. Letters are seldom lost.

The town of Chang Loh was much dilapidated. Yet there was a great deal of life in the streets. The inhabitants were busily occupied in making fine twine. Along the sides of the streets were most ingenious winding machines for twisting the hemp, some of them twisting from ten to twenty lines of twine, each line containing five strands of hemp.

In the neighbourhood of Chang Loh the soil is exceedingly fertile. All the plain is dotted with villages, and to the south are many market-towns of goodly size.

CHAPTER X.

The city of Tsingchow-foo—Its antiquity—Inns—Process of disin-
fection—A murder story—Falcons and falconry—Archers—A
walk through the city—Trades: silks, cutlery, calico printing—
Musicians—Chinese music—Maxims by ancient sages—Steam-
whistles in China—The manufacture of silk—A Tartar city.

WE reached Tsingchow-foo about noon. It is a departmental city of importance, and of great antiquity.
We entered by the east gate, but found there were no
inns in that quarter of the city. So we retraced our
steps, and went outside the wall to reach the north
gate, by which we went in. In one of the streets my
husband got a most kindly greeting from a pleasant,
bright-faced man. Inns were very few. After traversing a great part of the city, we went into one—a low,
musty-smelling place. It was very damp; so we lit
small fires of straw all over the floor. We were glad
even to shut in the smoke, to help in freshening up the
atmosphere.

A former traveller had deposited a large parcel of
salted fish on the floor. The odour left from them was
so very strong that I tried to avoid that corner of our
Tsingchow-foo domicile. An old woman who came in
gave another account of the disagreeable odour. Her
tale was this:—'One evening two travellers arrived
late and had supper. After everything was arranged

for the night the younger of the two tapped at the
landlord's room, and asked if he would take payment,
as they found they must start before daybreak. The
landlord did so, and noticed that they had had a great
deal of wine at supper. In the morning the stable-boy
was roused by a tap outside his window, and a voice
said, "You close the door; we are off." This was in the
autumn. No more was thought of the two travellers
till nearly six months after. Ever and anon some
traveller would complain of the foul odour of the place.
The dog at the inn began to scratch up the earth in a
corner under a wooden bedstead. At length the men
at the inn removed the bedstead to repair the damage,
and were horrified to find that the dog had scratched a
hole deep enough to disclose the putrifying remains of
a human hand. At once they went to the magistrate's
bureau. In full state the Chi-foo came and had the
whole exhumed. A small boy at the inn was sharp
enough to identify some ornament on the shoes as those
worn by the travellers who were supposed to have left
the inn very early one morning about six months before.
The body found was interred by order of the magistrates.
Nothing had transpired to lead to the identification
either of the dead man or his murderer.' I did not
like the inn any the better for the old woman's story.

One bit of beauty lit up this dismal, foul-smelling
room. It was an exquisite water-colour painting of a
white ger-falcon on a perch, with silken cord and tassels
thrown over a finely embroidered belt. The artist must
have been a lover of birds, or he never could have
given the life-like touch to this one. A good deal of
falconry is indulged in here. It is astonishing how
successful the falcons are in capturing their quarry.

They are carried on the wrist and hooded, as in the olden time. Indeed, this city has altogether an old-world look. We saw a great many archers. Two of them, with bows slung over their shoulders, came to our inn the first day we were there, begging medicine for a man who had got an arrow into his arm as the soldiers were practising archery outside the Manchu city. Robin Hood and Little John, I called them. One was tall and burly, the other short and slender. They were clad in olive-green.

We had crowds of people all day to talk to. In the evening we walked out, and found that the city, which supplies a large district, had been improved very much since the famine time. There were many fine streets in it. One street, which I dubbed Sheffield Street, seemed almost entirely filled with shops for cutlery goods. There were scissors, knives, swords, all sorts of steel implements and tools for various trades. The people trading in them were all as busy as possible, hammering, filing, welding, and riveting. In another street there seemed nothing but silk shops. In a third street many men were busily block-printing in colours, laying one colour on after the other very expeditiously. In another quarter men were brushing the patterns on over perforated vellum, and laying one colour over the other.

The people were most friendly. An old man offered to give us some music on an instrument called a *san hien*, a kind of guitar. He had evidently a musical taste, as he performed with some skill. His instrument had only three strings, and some of the music from it was wonderfully sweet. The crowd around him thought he was a first-rate player, and were most anxious that we should hear him play. After a time he asked us to

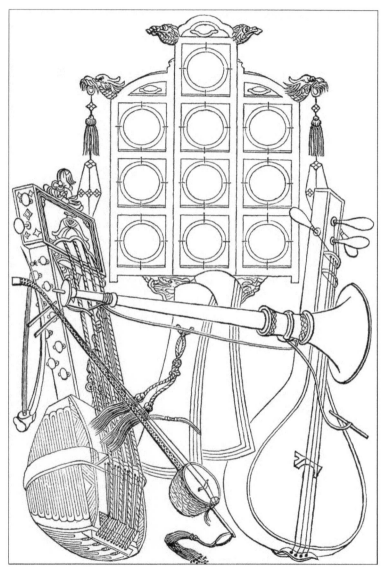

CHINESE MUSICAL INSTRUMENTS.

(From a Chinese Engraving.)

listen to a tune on the *ur hien,* a violin with two strings. He played a well-known Chinese tune, the 'Mo lee Wha.' But we thought that the *ur hien* was much shriller and harsher than the *san hien.* At other places on the journey we heard the Chinese play what is really their best instrument, the *cheng.* In this curious instrument, which is a rudimentary organ, there is a large bowl or cup, containing pipes of various lengths. In each of these pipes there is inserted a metallic tongue. The tubes or pipes have holes, to be covered and uncovered by the fingers. The mouth-piece is at the side. Some of the tunes played on this pipe are so exactly like those heard from Scottish bagpipes that, if we had not known them to be genuine Chinese airs, we should certainly have believed that some Alister MacAlister was operating on his national instrument. The Chinese *cheng* is not so overpowering as the Scottish bagpipe, and has some beautiful notes.

The Chinese have a great deal of printed music. They write their music all in the pentatonic scale, though at times they do introduce a fourth and a seventh, which they call convenient notes. They have also a kind of harp from which good music can be got. They profess to pay much attention to music, but the result is not very satisfactory. We thanked the old man for his kindly wish to entertain us; and he succeeded, for the tunes he played on the *san hien* were extremely pleasing.

In one of their old Taoist books mention is made of a great officer of state whose success was attributed to his musical powers. It is said of him, 'that music, morals, and the art of government, formed the triple cord wherewith he sought to secure the well-being of the State.' His teaching on these subjects was un-compromising. The three were indissolubly associated in his mind.

'When affairs cannot be carried on to success,' Confucius said, 'proprieties and music will not flourish. When proprieties and music do not flourish, punishments will not be properly awarded. It is by the Odes that the mind is aroused; it is by the rules of propriety that the character is established; it is from music that the finish is received.'

These two philosophers were musicians; the former, Chuang Tsze, considered that no coarse or vulgar person had any right to intermeddle with this divine accomplishment. His remark is: 'If a man be without the virtues proper to humanity, what has he to do with music?' This was written nearly two thousand years before Shakespeare penned the words:

> 'The man who hath not music in his soul
> Is fit for wars, stratagems, and treasons.'

One thing seemed very fashionable in Tsingchow too, viz. a gigantic hot-water kettle, with a compartment for fire, and a funnel going up through the kettle. A copper coin was so placed in the kettle that, when the water boiled, the hole in the coin, a cash, made a regular steam-whistle.[1] These were whistling on all sides, as it was just the time when the people prepared their evening meal. One and another rushed to the hot-water kettle to have tea infused. We, from our inn, patronised one of these kettles for all the hot water we required. The charge for a teapotful was not quite one farthing.

---

[1] The copper coins in use in China have all a hole in the centre, and are strung on a cord.

It was amusing to notice the varieties of teapots brought out by the inhabitants of Tsingchow-foo; they were of all sizes, shades, and shapes, round, square, hexagonal, large enough for twenty, and small enough for two.

The most important industry in the city is the preparation of silk. In all the district around Tsingchow-foo the silkworm is reared. Under foreign auspices this trade has revived and extended wonderfully. Every year thousands of bushels of cocoons are brought to the port of Chefoo. These are wound and spun at a large silk manufactory recently erected by foreigners. Under skilled treatment the silk of the Tsingchow-foo district is made most valuable for use in Europe, whither it is sent chiefly in the form of reeled yarn. Over a great part of the province of Shan-tung, and especially in the neighbourhood of Tsingchow-foo, this trade is a great blessing, as it gives employment to thousands of women and girls who would otherwise be destitute.

Just outside the wall of Tsingchow-foo there is a Tartar city, not large, but with a good wall, that has lately been carefully repaired. In former times there had been a wide moat surrounding the wall. Now it is dry, and is used for drilling the soldiers, and for practice with the large bow and arrow. This Tartar city is entirely a city of soldiers; no trade is done in it. The only shops in it are for victuals. The Tsingchow-foo people dislike the Tartar soldiers very much. As we passed in the early morning the whole place looked peaceful. All round the Tartar city wall the trees were waving green, and in full leaf. In this neighbourhood is a large number of native Christians.

F

CHAPTER XI.

A Chinese bride—Bridal privileges—Bridal attire—The return of a
bride to the house of her parents—Betrothal: when and how—
Sacredness—Marriages are made in heaven—A famous Chinese
story in illustration thereof.

ONE of many kind and thoughtful laws of China is that,
at the end of a few months, a newly wedded woman has
the privilege of visiting her parents' home. In Shan-
tung this law is almost always observed. The husband's
friends are usually willing, but if they object to take
the trouble, the elders of the village can compel them
to convey the bride to her mother's home in proper form
for this lawful visit.

As I journey on, along the old highway, there is
a ripple of silvery laughter, a trot, trot, of tiny hoofs,
hurrying to pass my shendzle. What a bonny, laughing face looks into mine!—large, lustrous, almond-
shaped eyes, and features, not Romanesque, yet perfect.
The lovely little rosebud mouth shows teeth as pearly
as can be boasted by any of Beauty's daughters in
Western lands. She is too old to be afraid, and too young
to be prudish. She has for escort a nice-looking lad
about fourteen years of age—a brother; the kinship
is written in their faces.

I give her a smile. She turns away with a blush
and another ripple of silvery laughter. She tries to

hurry the little donkey on, then changes her mind quickly, and says to her brother, ' You need not be in a great hurry.' Then another look. I keep my eyes fixed on my work, as I know she is taking a good look at me. Evidently she has not the least idea that I may understand her language; for in the prettiest Chinese she informs her brother, ' She has yellow hair, and a purple butterfly at her throat, and it is resting on a silver leaf.' This purple butterfly is a bow of satin ribbon.

' Can you see her feet ? '

' No, they are under the quilt.'

' Do you think she will have red shoes ? '

' No,' says the boy indignantly ; ' she is old.'

Then I look up. Again she blushes, and I have time to examine her dress; and, as it is typical, I will describe it.

Most important of all in the eyes of a Chinese bride are her shoes, so there I must begin. What radiant shoes they are—of glistening rose-pink satin, worked in shaded blue silk embroidery, intermingled with gold! The outlines of the shoes are in fine gold braid, and just at the instep can be seen the tiniest bit of white—the bandage with which her foot is bound. The sole of that little foot would not much more than cover the length of my palm. Round the ankle is a small gaiter of sea-green silk, tied with a red silk ribbon two inches wide, and with tassels at the hanging ends. The little foot is most artistically displayed under her riding skirt of scarlet cloth. This skirt is made in gores, about six inches wide at the hem, and tapering to the waist. Each gore is bound with black satin, and the scarlet cloth is profusely covered with shaded blue embroidery, butterflies being predominant.

Sitting straight on the back of the donkey, her elaborate riding skirt can be fully seen, it being spread out over the saddle-bags, which hang well over the sides of the animal. She wears a loose jacket of crimson brocaded crape, the long sleeves draping most gracefully. The jacket has a black satin binding, and a trimming of white satin about two inches wide, beautifully embroidered in blue and gold. Then an immense collar in arabesques, bound with black satin, and embroidered with various hues. Just where the sleeves form a line from the shoulders, there hang two magnificent tassels of scarlet and blue and gold. The little hands that hold the reins are gloveless, but they are white and shapely. Her head-dress is a broad band, mysterious in its beauty of satin and embroidery. This also is bound with black satin, and, straight up the forehead, studded with gems like small brooches. Her earrings are a mass of slender chains of gold, with blue enamel pendants, like a miniature chatelaine; each earring, though light, would be almost a handful, and has this advantage, that it 'makes music wherever she goes.' Her jet black hair is smooth and glossy, put up in a coil behind, and fastened with many and most variedly ornamental gold pins. There are a few balls of crimson silk at the left side.

Crimson is China's bridal colour; for brides in China are all royal, an empress in ancient times having granted them that privilege.

Whilst taking note of the lady's dress I have also been observing the kindliness existing between the rider and her little squire. That boy loves his sister; affection is seen in his every look. He has dressed the little white donkey to bring her home. There is a bit of

red cord tying up its tail, a red rosette at each ear, and
its head-gear is all brilliant with twists of scarlet braid.
They turn up a cross road leading to a village shaded
by fine elm trees, and looking lovely in the morning
sunlight. On the edge of the village is a handsome
house. Near the house is a group of boys and girls in
gay clothing. As the little donkey trots up the road
I see demonstrations of joy among the band. The
blues and scarlets of their robes are intermingling like
a fairy show. Evidently there is a merry greeting for
the two, who, forgetting the foreigner, are urging the
little donkey to his utmost speed. I can hear the
shouts of the children, though I cannot distinguish
their words. A tall, handsome Chinaman comes out of
the house, just in time to take the beauty into his arms ;
and I am mistaken if that father does not clasp his
daughter with as much affection as is bestowed on
daughters in Western lands.

'Marriages are made in heaven'; no nation believes
this more firmly than the Chinese. The formalities
necessary to a marriage are gone through in the gravest
manner. In every town and village there are women
who gain a livelihood by attending to these matters.
The precise time of a child's birth is always noted by
the family, as that on which depend all the future
events in its life.

Betrothal is arranged for by the *pronuba* or go-
between. The family of the young man is supposed to take
the initiative. The first act is to give the go-between
a card with the family name, the hour, day, month,
and year of the birth of the prospective bridegroom.
This card is presented to the match-maker who acts on
behalf of an eligible young lady. A card giving the

same information about her is presented to the match-maker on behalf of the young man. The two match-makers consult Zadkiel. If he pronounces favourably regarding the proposed match, then the details of the betrothal are arranged.

One Chinese law of marriage is that no persons bearing the same family name may be betrothed. This prohibition has been in force from early times. In course of ages it happened that whole communities came to have the same family name, so that men had often to make long and expensive journeys to get wives. This became so oppressive that in the years between A.D. 1403 and A.D. 1425, during the reign of the emperor Yung Lo, a law was enacted that members of families who had military titles, and families who were strictly private people, though having the same name, might intermarry.

In China only the heads of families are interested in the making of marriages. The young men and women themselves are not likely ever to meet prior to their wedding-day. Indeed, the Chinese idea of a happy union is, that the couple do not see each other till after the wedding, when it is the custom for the bridegroom to lead his bride into his mother's apartment. He there unveils her, and for the first time looks in the face of the woman with whom he is to spend his life.

In spite of early betrothals, there is a great amount of domestic happiness in China. No feelings of injustice and no ideas of forced marriage are associated with the ancient and universal custom.

While the details of betrothal are in process, it is believed that if the marriage is not registered in heaven, the Heavenly Father will interfere to interrupt it. So betrothal has to run the gauntlet of circumstances. If anything unlucky happen in either family while arrangements are in process, even so small an event as the breaking of a piece of crockery or the loss of any article of value, the negotiations would be stopped and the cards returned. However, should the 'course of betrothal run smooth,' the horological card is produced, and two threads of scarlet silk and four long and large needles. These needles are solemnly threaded at each end of the threads. Two of these needles are passed through the card in the possession of the bridegroom's family, and sent to the family of the bride. The other two needles are passed through the card in possession of the bride's family. These cards are kept most carefully as evidence of the betrothal being binding.

All the documents relating to a marriage are written out in front of the ancestral tablet. Until the whole process is legalised the cards are deposited under the incense vase in front of the tablet. The phrase used in declaring a betrothal completed is, 'The red strings are tied.'

I may relate the story on which this is based. It is constantly told by the legend-loving :—In the Tang dynasty, A.D. 618–905, a student went to the capital of the province for his B.A. examination. He had worked so hard and become so anxious that he could not sleep. One fine moonlight night he walked out to the lake beside the city wall. There he observed an old man reading a book by the light of the moon. 'What are you studying?' said the young student. 'The book of matches for all places under the heavens;' adding, 'I always carry about with me the cords with which to tie those who ought to be united; and when this cord is tied nothing can change it; the two will come together, even though they are at the extremes of the earth. You will see your future wife in the home of the old woman who sells vegetables at the north of the lake. The cord is tied.' Next day the student found the shop and the old woman. She had a young girl in her arms. He thought the girl would be ugly like her mother; so he hired a ruffian to kill the girl. The student was told that the ruffian had killed her. No one cared, for the woman was poor. Fourteen years afterwards, when the student had become a mandarin, and many attempts at marriage had failed, his superior officer gave him his daughter in marriage. She was very beautiful, but always wore her head-dress with an ornament over her left eyebrow. Her husband asked her why she wore this ornament. She said, 'When I was a little girl, my old nurse carried me out in the street, and one day a robber struck me. The old woman and I fell down on the stones, and she thought I was dead, but she bound up the wound, and I recovered. The scar of the wound is still here.' She pushed off her head-dress and showed the mark of what must have been a frightful wound. 'I am the prefect's niece,' she continued. 'My father died in the Sung, and my old nurse, who sold vegetables, took me to her home till my uncle could send for me.'

CHAPTER XII.

Chinese marriages: their antecedents and formalities—The bride passes through a trying ordeal—A Chinese woman-hater—How he trained his son: his precautions, and the result.

In rich Chinese families the wedding trousseau is often a matter of vanity and parade. I have seen a wedding outfit borne by more than a hundred coolies, and all the articles tied with red silk crape to the carrying poles. Before a trousseau is sent off everything in it is 'sifted,' so that no evil influences may go from the house of the bride. On the day previous to the wedding, the bride's parents invite their friends to a feast. The bride is dressed in her wedding robes, and her hair is done up in the style of a married woman. While friends are feasting the bride goes through her farewell ceremonies. She lights incense before the ancestral tablets of her father's house, and worships there for the last time. She kneels down before her grandparents, her father and mother, also her aunts and uncles, and worships them. It is really a formal leave-taking, and is often very sad. This is done after the bridal chair, usually sent the day before the wedding, has arrived.

On the morning of the wedding-day she is called 'The new woman,' and is invested with a large and magnificently embroidered veil of scarlet crape, having a blue and gold crown over it. This veil completely conceals her features, and almost her form. Preceded by musicians, and amid the firing of crackers, she is borne away. Everything in the procession is crimson—dress, chair, lanterns. These lanterns have printed on them the family name of the bride. From the bridegroom's home a procession goes forth to convey the bride. When the bearers of the lanterns in the two processions meet, they gyrate round each other; those carrying the name of the bridegroom take their places in front of the chair. From that time the bride's name is changed, and her lantern-bearers with her name, and her part of the procession, return to her home, where the women of the house are supposed to be wailing in great grief.

Wedding ceremonies are under the supervision of the priests, and in connection with them are the worshippings of both gods and men, and many superstitious practices. At the wedding ceremony the pair are placed before an altar prepared in the reception room. The bride is so completely blindfolded by the thick veil that she has to be led about. The heralds blow a blast. The priests chant some sentences. The musicians play their loudest. When the din has reached a climax, the pair kneel and worship heaven, earth, and the bridegroom's ancestors. The assistants produce from the altar two cups filled with wine, tied together with a crimson silk cord. The bridegroom sips a little from one; the other is put to the bride's lips, the veil intervening. The two cups of wine are then intermingled. The ends of the sashes are tied together, and the bridegroom leads his bride into his mother's room.

CHINESE COUPLE LATELY MARRIED.

There is a little by-play as they take their seats together on a sofa. Each endeavours to sit on a portion of the other's dress, as it is supposed that the one whose dress is sat upon will be sure to get the worst of it all through life. After this the groom unveils his bride.

During the whole evening the bride is exhibited. Every one who chooses may go in and have a look at her, as she stands up on exhibition. She must not speak, or laugh, or scarcely move, but remain like a waxwork figure, while people make remarks on her general appearance. This is a most fatiguing and un-refined ordeal, especially after a long journey and all the excitements of the day. I was once called in to help a poor young bride who had fainted away; and after she was restored to consciousness there was some difficulty in clearing the house of spectators.

But, with all these tedious formalities, young China-men are quite apt to fall in love. Ofttimes it happens that a betrothed dies. Then, if the young man is grown up, he has a chance of quietly looking about him, and by some old aunt or other person get a marriage to his liking arranged. Some of the most popular Chinese songs relate such adventures. If he is a very aspiring young man, and has taken a good literary degree, he may in the large card which every graduate is allowed to paste up insert an advertisement, saying that he is willing to become the son-in-law of a rich man. This is frequently done by poor but fortunate students. Many a rich man who has no literary standing keeps a favourite daughter unbetrothed, in hope of getting a literary graduate for a son-in-law. Of course the young man takes the ancestral name of his father-in-law, and is always spoken of as a son, while the daughter is spoken of as though she were another man's daughter. Thus the rich can burnish their gold with the coveted sheen and glory of literature

The following legend is told :—A man had an only son whom he loved very dearly. He had a good sum of money, which he put out to interest, and retired, with his son, to a house on the top of a mountain. As the father was a literary man, he taught his son. The boy became fond of literature, and particularly fond of ornamental writing and drawing. For many years the father and son lived in complete happiness. The father made journeys down the mountain to the neighbouring town for necessaries. He was careful to supply his son most liberally with drawing materials. As age crept on, and he was no longer able to carry their household supplies up the mountain, his son dutifully entreated for leave to descend the mountain along with him. He reluctantly consented, and several trips were made. One morning, as they got to the town they found a theatrical company there, attracting crowds to the usually quiet place. Suddenly there appeared on the road, hurrying to the theatre, three lovely young girls, dressed to perfection.

' What are these ? ' exclaimed the son.

' Don't look at them,' said his father; ' they are devils.' But the son could not withdraw his eyes from a sight so wonderful.

On their way up the mountain the boy plied his father with all manner of questions about the apparitions. The father was full of stories of the disasters people had suffered through having anything to do with such dreadful creatures, and of the frightful evils which would result from even thinking of them. In awe-struck

tones the father told his son that, if he did not wish
to be separated from his father for evermore, he must
not again speak of them.

So they got home, and matters went on as usual,
though not quite as usual; for the son took to going
out alone, and lying in the sun, with his hat over his
eyes. He took less interest in his drawings, and none
in his books. His little dog got no attention, so that
it preferred staying by the old man, while he cultivated
their little patch of vegetables. Matters became worse
and worse. The son scarcely ever spoke to his father,
but went solitarily about. His father feared he was ill,
and anxiously asked him to see a doctor. In their visits
to the town he noticed that his son always loitered as
long as possible. Suddenly the young man took to his
pencils and paints, and worked hard at some secret work,
always carefully locking up his little sanctum. Then
again he became listless. His father was most solicitous,
and once got up in the night to look. The light was
burning in his son's sanctum, the door open. Noiselessly
he slipped in, and there sat his son, as pale as death,
before the picture of a beautiful Chinese lady. The son
became aware of his father's presence, and, rising, threw
himself into his arms, exclaiming, "Oh! father, that
tallest devil!'

CHAPTER XIII:

In the course of our travels we came to a town where
a great *whei*, or religious festival, was being held. Guests
were so numerous that, after travelling all over the town,
we were driven to take shelter at an inn which has such
an unenviable reputation, that Chinese who know the
place would rather trudge on by night or camp out
than risk staying at it. We had no alternative. By
representation of the muleteers, who said the inn had
changed hands, and was now in charge of very respectable people, we were induced to go in. When we first
arrived in the town the ostlers were all at the inn gate,
and almost forced us to go in. However, after a vain
search for another place we were obliged to return and
enter.

I was entertained afterwards with tales of lonely
travellers who had disappeared at that inn. We found
it really deserved a bad name. In the morning the
keepers of the inn insisted on being paid more than
three times the proper amount. On our refusing to pay

it, every man flew to his sword. A veritable set of ruffians they were. While they were arming, we walked right out and along to the high road, where there were, though early, already many travellers. When the scoundrels saw that we were gone, they took the amount (twice as much as they ought to have had), and allowed our mules to come after us.

At this place there was a great theatre, built of matting, and most tastefully decorated. As we passed in the early morning, the play had not commenced. It is considered quite a meritorious act to give a play. The actors are all paid by one rich man. The stage is erected in a large open place, generally in front of a temple. No charge is made for admission. All who can get standing room may go. The respectable plays are principally from historical subjects. Some of the actors are of great merit, from a Chinese point of view, and become such favourites that they command large sums of money. In the historical plays, they are very careful to be in the costume proper to the time. They depend almost entirely for effect on costume. To the other accessories of the stage, such as 'scenes,' they pay almost no attention.

So far as I can learn, the Chinese have no passion-drama, such as the 'Muharram' of the Persians, and nothing at all in character like the tragedy of 'Husain.' They are fond of emperors and courts. The religious element does not enter into their plays. Power is the keynote of all Chinese theatricals. Women are not allowed to act on the Chinese stage. Young boys always take the parts of women. Yet in their plays they are fond of having many female representations. The acting of the Chinese does not rise to the dignity

G

of art; and I have never heard that they cater for tears. I was once privileged, in a private manner, to see one of their finest companies of actors. They chose an historical play, or rather a kind of opera; for there was a great deal of singing, and the orchestra accompanied in a marvellously unharmonious concord. The story came out well, and some of the actors, under good training, would have been above the average stage-player.

At Chang San Hien we made our mid-day halt. The town is very dilapidated; we had great difficulty in getting quiet in which to eat our luncheon. Dr. Williamson had frequently to go out to clear a space in front of the door.

As usual, numbers of women crowded round the shendzle. Bright and pleasant they looked. We had a nice little chat with some of them after dinner. One bright young mother placed her baby, of whom she was evidently very proud, in my lap, and said, ' Now you can have him.' The little fellow smiled up into my face, not in the least afraid. How beautiful motherhood is! The one thought of that young Chinese mother was that precious baby, and this was a little trick to get him into notice. I patted and praised him, and the mother blushed, and beamed with perfect sunshine on her face. The women were all exceeding friendly, and one and another, as I passed out, said, ' When will you come back again? When will you come back? Come soon.'

In this inn-yard I saw two women police. The Chinese have at all their magistrates' offices women who assist in the duties of the court. In rural districts they have women who are entrusted with the duty of helping to keep the peace, and who have a right to interfere in the cause of justice. Western lands have thought of many places that women might fill to advantage. Has any one suggested women police? These 'Ya-Men' women are easily known. They are generally in the prime of life—from thirty-five to forty-five— usually of a tall and strong build, and very loud-voiced. When they come into an inn-yard they salute the landlord or the muleteers. They are women of good character, but their position is not envied. I should have said they are always widows, and are in this service with consent of the parents of their late husbands. Recognised by law, there are also lady doctors.

The town is now very wretched, and dilapidated in the extreme. Long years ago it must have been rather a pretty place. In its palmy days many *pei-lows* had been built. In the centre of the town there was a very old one. I notice that in the oldest *pei-low* the lions are either crouching with outstretched paws or seated with paws close together. The figure of the lion as an architectural accessory has been imported into China. The Chinese name for a lion is a foreign word of Persian origin. Usually Chinese artists are fairly correct in their representation of animals, but they always decorate the lion with a mane all down his spine to the root of his tail. On the newer *pei-low* the lions are seated, sometimes half profile, grinning at each other. Under the paw there is usually a ball or the globe. Sometimes they are fondling a tiny cub.

All along the street men were reeling silk outside their doors. The reels were tiny things, prettily made. The largest I saw was about three feet long. The skeins of silk were just a fraction over fifty inches,

measuring all round.   One skein given to me must have
been wound on a very large winder, as it measured
two hundred and two inches round.   The silk was of
a most exquisite yellow, the real 'old gold' that ladies
have of late thought so becoming.   I thought how that
silk might perchance be woven into robes for ladies
in England.   We are linked each to each all over
the world.   The noble dame who may sweep through
stately halls in a robe made of this silk knows little of
the land whence it comes—how fair are its scenes and
how sunny its skies.   Little can she know of the host
of workers that have contributed to produce the glossy
fabric she so much admires.   I wish I could photo-
graph for her the lovely Chinese maids and matrons
who tend the silkworms, the bright-eyed cherubs who
gather the leaves for the food of the worms, the thousand and one pictures of calm domestic life in the
homes of these people.   And I would ask those who
dwell in the lordly halls of England to provide the
means of training the minds and bringing the comfort
of the Gospel to the hearts of those Chinese who con-
tribute so much to the adorning of the persons of
England's fair daughters.   I always found that in the
districts where the silkworms are raised the people were
more refined, and certainly the women were more elegant and more intelligent than in districts where the
crops are only cereals.

CHAPTER XIV.

JUST outside the town of Chang San Hien there is a beautiful piece of water, crossed by a long, flat, stone bridge. At intervals, on the outside of the parapet, are gargoyles, the water running off from the open mouths of finely carved dragons' heads. At the west end of this bridge there is a temple, though now neglected and fast becoming a ruin. When first built, it must have been very imposing. There could hardly be a finer site. The water spreads out in front of it, and it is surrounded by a raised embankment, with an ornamental stone parapet. All around the plain is well wooded. The roads are avenues of fine elm, beech, and willow trees. In the distance the hills from which the place takes its name (' Long Hill Town ') have soft, flowing outlines, and its blue is as intense as the blue of the sky, but in tint a little deeper.

We bade farewell to Chang San Hien, thinking that much kindliness to foreigners existed amongst the people.

Tseu Ping Hien is a town full of *pei-lows*. One in the centre of the town is of great beauty. It is very ancient; the people around could not tell how old it was—an immense mass of stone, that spoke volumes for the skill of the architects. Artistic talent was displayed in the carvings; some of the little pieces in panels, executed in relief in stone, being really good. This *pei-low* was jointed in the stone throughout, no mortar having been used; all the great slabs were grooved and dovetailed into each other.

These *pei-lows* are really triumphal gateways, and they have a most imposing effect. They span the road usually in three divisions, a wide space in the centre and two smaller at the sides. They vary from twenty to over sixty feet high. Usually there are ornamental panels on them, and sometimes the story of a hero is cut in relief in white marble. At the base are often the lions that the Chinese are so fond of representing in stone. Surrounding the foot of this one in Tseu Ping Hien were no fewer than sixteen stone lions, eight on either side. These lions were all couching with outstretched paws.

If one is stopped in a Chinese street, he is apt to say to himself, 'What an immense number of people with nothing to do!' Although the Chinese as a nation are industrious, yet it is surprising how many of them all their lives do absolutely nothing.

A great fair or market was being held, and plenty of ready money going in it—not as in the little country fair of which we have spoken. There seemed to be for sale everything necessary for Chinese humanity, from silk to soap.

It is hard to picture out before the reader a city

A CITY MARKET OR FAIR.

(*From a Chinese drawing.*)

street more than a mile in length, lined on both sides
with stalls, on which are displayed all things for use or
ornament. Further to the west, vegetables and grain
are sold : these are displayed on matting spread on the
raised pathway at each side of the street. The sellers
at these fairs pay a tax to the town. There were few
women in the market ; but a Chinaman has a very good
idea of the requirements of his household.

The articles displayed at this market—and it was a
regular one—gave us a good insight into the condition
and comfort of the district. Vegetables and fruits of
many kinds were there. Grain was abundant, and in
great variety. There were many kinds of matting,
some of it quite gay in designs of white and scarlet.
There were baskets, brooms, crockery, shoes, incense
papers, silk, yellow and white, cotton in pod, and
spun yarn, native cloth of all colours, and great piles
of what in England is called Nanking cloth. There
were tables of cakes and confections, tables of fortune-
tellers and letter-writers, perambulating soup-kitchens
and peripatetic barbers, mobs of mules and donkeys,
salt and sugar-cane, gossiping ducks and gobbling
geese, hens and mocking-birds, imitating all manner of
sounds. There were firewood and charcoal, fir cones and
fir branches. What a strange mingling of all sorts of
things was there under the bluest of blue skies, under a
vault of heaven having a look of height that I have
never seen elsewhere !

Some of the stalls dazzled with sham jewellery,
bracelets and pins, earrings, all the gewgaws that girls
like, with a little box in a corner having a pair or two
of real gold and gem earrings, worth more than all the
sparkling show. There were books and artificial flowers,

and blooming flowers and flowering shrubs. As we afterwards went along the road, we were greeted with the exquisite perfume of the *kwe hwa*, and saw men carrying flowers and shrubs in all directions from the market.

In the midst of all the traffic of the fair our shen-dzles halted, and our books were taken out. A rapid sale began. The concourse of people became so great that the way was blocked up; so we had to leave the booksellers behind, and go straight through the main street to the outskirts of the town, where there was room to unload the poor animals.

Hither there was a great rush of little-footed China! I was making an attempt to sell books, but saw it would be dangerous, as I was in dread lest any of the little children might be trampled to death. It was interesting to me to see the efforts the men made so that their women-folk might see the foreign woman. Stools were borrowed and forms were hired from neighbouring shops, and women and girls stood on them, held up by fathers, husbands, and brothers. A murmur ran round the crowd, 'She speaks our tongue.' Then I was plied with questions. I mounted on the poles of the shendzle; that raised me over the heads of the crowd. Only women and girls were near. Boys and men were on the outskirts. So I told them of my reason for coming to China, and said that I had some-thing to teach women. Immediately my voice was heard there was a stillness over that great assembly. A doctrine for women was new to them. A person come to exhort women to be good, to avoid lying, to curb their tempers and put a bridle on their tongues, to pray to the Heavenly Father, and to reverence His

Son, our Lord and Saviour, to worship the Heavenly Father in their own homes, to raise an altar for Him in their hearts, not to go to temples and worship and burn incense to idols, and to believe that in heaven there was a place prepared for Chinese women.

The men nodded their heads, saying, ' Good,' ' That's right.' The women said, ' True.' Then a pause and a change of audience, and the address was repeated. Not once was an objectionable word used. All were kindly polite. Some invited me into their houses, but I declined, and told them I feared the difficulty they would have in keeping out the crowd. Many of them said, ' You.will come back soon.'

A fine private cart, equal to a good carriage at home, was drawn up near enough to hear. In it was seated a lady who had a teapot in a basket-work cosy. She got it filled with hot water at an inn on the opposite side of the road. In a short time she sent her little daughter in the arms of a serving man, the child bearing a cup of tea with some sweetmeats in the saucer. It was a ladylike act to offer the first cup to the stranger. The tea was a most grateful refreshment in the midst of all the heat and dust. Over the heads of the crowd I, from my perch, bowed, or rather shook my hands, in acknowledgment of the kindness. The lady answered the salaam. When I had finished the tea I returned the cup to the child, and presented her with a small pictorial magazine. Her mother evidently feared the child had not thanked me, so she made her return in the arms of the servant, and, in the prettiest way imaginable, the little girl put her hands together and thanked me. She was dressed in a beautiful pale green silk jacket, with black satin arabesques, scarlet trousers, and pink shoes. It looked as if the man had captured a gigantic tropical butterfly.

After some time the booksellers arrived, followed by an immense crowd. In a little while we mounted our shendzles and set off, amid much noise and excitement, and a great rushing for a final purchase of books. The people were all kindly disposed. My husband seemed to be well known amongst them.

As we went out of the town, troops of women and children gathered at various points to see us pass. Many Chinese gentlemen came to purchase books, so that my husband had to get out of his shendzle to supply them.

On entering or leaving a Chinese city you can form a good idea of its size by the number of the graves that lie immediately outside its walls. These are chiefly the graves of the poor and of strangers. In the eleventh century there was quite a rage for cremation. At first the priests, for the benefit of the poor, encouraged the practice, as they said ' the poor could not afford the expense of sepulture '; but by-and-by they began to cremate the rich also, and to appropriate to themselves the legacies that ought to have been devoted to ancestral worship. The priests made great gain by it, and much valuable property passed into their hands. In A.D. 1157 the Chinese Government forbade cremation, and set apart cemeteries for the poor. However, the priests still persisted in cremating; and by this acquired property in temples that they still retain. In the year A.D. 1261 a petition was presented to the throne for the prohibition of the erection of furnaces for cremation. This was earnestly sought, as cremation interfered materially with the rites of ancestral worship, and was only encouraged by the priests to cover their peculations. The petition was granted. Buddhist priests of high standing are still cremated, and the law permits the coffin of an unknown stranger to be burned, especially if it has been lying exposed for a long time and is decayed. It is legally burned, and the ashes spread about.

The Chinese are not materialists. They have a very marked belief in the existence of the soul after death. Each grave mound we have passed tells this ; for at the present season, spring-time, the graves have each a beautiful square-cut sod laid on the top, to signify that spring has come.

We met on the road an immense cavalcade conveying a large coffin from Peking. The coffin was a very handsome one covered with bright blue Russian cloth and trimmed with gilding. The pall was crimson Russian cloth, hanging about six inches over the coffin. Over all was an almost transparent oiled silk cover. On the top, in a wicker cage, was a white cock leading a most happy life. From the top of this cage floated a triangular flag of yellow satin, bearing in black characters the titles of the deceased. On a piece of yellow satin at the head of the coffin was a long list of the virtues of the dead mandarin. This was carried by four handsome mules, the largest I have seen. The cock is never absent from the carrying of a coffin from one place to another. The Chinese believe that this fowl has a special influence in inducing the spirit to follow the body.

It is the wish of every Chinaman to be 'gathered to his fathers,' to sleep his last long sleep in the little yew-shaded graveyard where all his people lie. The bodies of the very greatest men of the empire are often thus transported to be laid to rest near some obscure little village.   There is no Westminster Abbey or St. Paul's Cathedral for the Chinaman who has served his country. The Chinese have more faith in the family than in the nation.

CHAPTER XV.

On leaving Tseu Ping Hien, after a short ride in the early morning, we passed Chang Kieu. Outside of the wall to the east we saw four fine and very large waterwheels in motion. There is abundant water power in this neighbourhood. We dined at a small place called Lee Tien, in an inn remarkable for dirt and festooned with venerable cobwebs. The country is very flat.

In all these towns and villages coal is used as fuel. The people looked dirtier than in other parts, and particularly the little children were smutty in the extreme. Along the streets there was to be seen the perambulating coalman, ringing a bell hung under his wheelbarrow, the rope attached to the handle, and shouting 'Coal! coal!' It seemed to be very cheap indeed, and was sold by measure in a great square wooden trough. When a purchase was made the coal merchant obligingly took hold of two of the handles of the trough, and helped the purchaser to carry the coal into his house.

Outside the town of Lee Tien we saw many wheelbarrow loads of queer, hexagonal-shaped straw hats, with ventilating crown-pieces. For convenience of carriage the hats were all packed together, while the crown-pieces were in bunches by themselves. These hats were most ingeniously woven, and were meant to serve as hat and umbrella in one.

The highway as we got near Tsi-nan-foo became wider, and the number of mules on the road was very

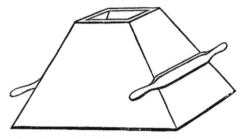

COAL MEASURE WITH HANDLES FOR CARRYING.

large. Indeed, it was a lively sight. There were a great many travellers. The constant greetings of friends and the chatter about local affairs were quite entertaining. We made a very short stage, and stopped at a place called Kwo Tien. It was some time before sunset, so we had leisure to inspect the room before we entered it. It was so dirty that we resolved to go elsewhere; rather than allow us to do this, the room received such a cleaning as it had not had for years, and was wholly refurnished to suit our convenience.

In the morning we feel that we are near the centre of civilisation, for we are to enter Tsi-nan-foo, the capital of the province. This is China's classic province, and is in reality a kingdom. In Scotland there are something under four millions of inhabitants. In Shantung there are something over thirty-three millions. There is in the province abundance of coal, iron, silver, lead, and all material for building purposes. Shantung has a splendid seaboard. It has a fine race of people, and boasts of being the birthplace of China's greatest sages.

As we get near the city we have a very fair specimen of the ' Old Highways.' They seem at present to have small attention from road committees; broad highways are left with the unrepaired ruts of many winters, waiting till some severe flood will smooth them over, to be again cut up by the wheels of busy traffic. The bridges also are seldom in repair, and are often inconveniently placed; yet we could not but admire the wondrous engineering skill which the builders of these bridges must have possessed.

In the cities the pariah dogs and the ubiquitous pig divide the duties of sanitation, with an occasional sweeping when the mud becomes like a liquid stream. When a foreigner complains of the condition of highway or street, the Chinese give a knowing look, as much as to say, ' If you don't like our roads, you can stay at home.'

On the highway there was quite a number of bullocks. Some of them were shod with iron, as of olden time in Rome oxen used to be shod. Some oxen had only straw sandals tied on each hoof. These they call ' five li shoes,' that is, they last only about a mile and three quarters. Oxen are much used for ploughing, and do their work steadily. Going towards Tsi-nan-foo

H

we were particularly struck by the straightness of the furrows on a piece of newly-ploughed land.

While we have been interested in highway and field, there has been looming into view the great Sentinel Hill, an isolated volcanic cone; this morning gleaming purple as an amethyst, and standing like a grand sentry to guard the capital of the province, the great city of Tsi-nan-foo.

Many years ago I made a visit to this city; and as it took place when the great triennial examination was being held, it may interest the reader if I give an account here of that most interesting visit.

We arrived just as the sun was setting in the west, and the handsome gateway and lofty crenelated wall were tinted with a glory of purple and gold. We drove through the fine wide streets, and turned into the spacious yard of an inn near the Mahommedan mosque. There were already some forty or fifty mules in the yard, many of them rolling over and over on the ground in high enjoyment at being relieved of their hot pack-saddles, others munching gratefully at their bran, beans, and straw. The whole place was alive with restless animals.

The inn itself was old and much dilapidated, though roomy and airy. There were several courtyards belonging to it; and ranged round these were many small rooms suited for students. These were all full, as fifteen thousand Bachelors of Arts had arrived in the city for examination. We were shown to a suite of rooms at the extreme north of the inn, where we had a chance of seeing a great many of these candidates for literary honours. They all seemed bright and intelligent fellows, very sedate, and anxiously discussing examination affairs. Students before their examination are sufficiently quiet

and subdued, but after the dread trial is over they are apt
to rush headlong into all sorts of wild practical jokes.
The mandarins are always excessively anxious regarding
the peace of the city as corps after corps is passed out
of the examiners' hands. The first batch were still in,
so we felt fairly safe.

Early the following morning we set out on foot to
explore the famous city. After being accustomed to the
squalor of little towns, Tsi-nan-foo looked to me the
Paris of China. The streets are very handsome, much
wider than the streets of cities in the South of China,
and they are well paved. In the business part of the
city the shops are very lofty and most handsome. Every
shop is wholly exposed by day, and is shut in at night
by immense boards. While the eaves are a mass of
lacquer and gilding, each shop seems to vie with its
neighbour in the amount and gorgeousness of the carving, gilding, and exquisite colouring of the sides and
cornices. Scarlet, green, black, and immense portiont
of gilt flash in the sunlight and dazzle one with the
brilliancy. Each shop has a counter running all along
the front. The tea and silk shops do not expose their
wares, but the counters are profusely decorated with
flowers in pots, and with dwarf trees full of blossom.
The restaurants, the fruit and confection shops display
their dainties to the best advantage, and most of them
are decorated with flowers. The attendants at the finer
shops are very numerous, and are usually young men
exceedingly well dressed and agreeable in their manners.

The most prominent buildings in Tsi-nan-foo are the
Roman Catholic cathedral, with its Western architecture
and glittering cross, and the Mahommedan mosque,
with its silver crescent. These two buildings prove that

religious toleration is granted, and they speak constantly to the students of teachings other than those of Confucius.

As the morning advanced the streets became more crowded ; but the people were civil, though they stared in utter amazement at the foreign woman, the first woman of a strange race that had ever trod their streets. If they showed any symptoms of crowding or jostling, a polite remark from me in their own tongue usually made them fall back into a respectful attitude, and from one to another would go the words, ' She speaks our language,' ' She understands our rites.'

After getting enough of the noise and heat of the streets, in the afternoon we made our way to the beautiful lake which is inside the city wall.   There were numberless pleasure boats waiting for hire.   In one of the most brilliantly painted we embarked and sailed softly over the shining lake.   It was perfect fairyland as we glided up one avenue and down another, for the lake is divided into portions, each separated by a floating artificial bank.   These divisions are most ingeniously arranged.   Anchored to stakes and large stones at the bottom of the lake are tiny wicker-work rafts.   On these rafts a quantity of sods and a stiff growth of reedy plants and some mould are piled up.   All are bound firmly together by the natural growth of the roots and fibres of plants.   On these banks are planted willows and other trees that thrive in damp soil, also endless varieties of water-loving plants and beautiful flowers, some of them almost tropical in their richness.   All this vegeta-tion was a pleasure to the eye.   The spaces enclosed were all radiant with pink lotus flowers and their beautifully shaped leaves.   I enjoyed sailing over these avenues of water and watching the men at this season busy harvesting these broad leaves, which are dried and used extensively for wrapping up parcels of grocery and other wares. The men gathering the lotus leaves were all paddling about in tubs. I asked why they did not take boats. They said tubs were better, as they did not injure either the lotus plants or the floating gardens.

As we sailed about, sometimes we came to a rocky island on which a series of pleasure palaces were built. In front of these was a large open space, where the pink and white lotus were growing in the loveliest luxuriance. It was just the time when all the loungers of gay Tsinan-foo enjoyed the luxury of afternoon tea in these handsome palaces. These palaces are public property, but many people seemed to make a trade of supplying tea to visitors. In the balmy air the gorgeous blossoms, the brilliant hues of the robes of the Tsi-nan-foo dandies, mixed with the soft whites and blues of the crape robes of the elderly scholars, were dazzling. I could scarcely believe that this was China. Surely we were under the spell of Aladdin, who is reported to have lived somewhere in this direction. We seated ourselves, and I watched a group of gay young Chinamen, some of them lounging over the stone balustrade in front of the palace. Regular aristocrats they were, and dressed in the most lustrous of brocaded silks or in the crimpiest of cream-coloured crapes, flirting their fans with admirable grace, talking, laughing, and thinking themselves the observed of all observers, too proud to seem anxious to stare at the foreigners, yet evidently most desirous to study these specimens of Western barbarism. To my eye, so long accustomed to the peasant Chinaman, the elegance of these lolling students was quite a treat.

After a most charming afternoon, near sunset, we

embarked again in our gaudy pleasure boat. Here and there, all over the water, was a beautiful aquatic plant, as if a handful of the leaves of the rose tree had been thrown at intervals all about. The sun set just as we were in sight of a fine temple where we meant to disembark. Suddenly the paddling at the stern of the boat ceased; a fine-toned bell tolled a few strokes; all the surrounding boats stopped; not a sound was heard. In the gathering gloom I could just descry a troop of men and another group dressed as young women, each attended by a priestess, and coming down the broad flight of steps. Suddenly, out from the steps floated a tiny spark of fire, that rose until it burned a steady flame. Then another and another, till the whole place was full of dancing lights. Some floated so near that we could see that they were the celebrated lotus lanterns, made of little wooden basins, each surrounded by a beautifully made and exquisitely coloured paper lotus flower. These basins were filled with melted tallow having a thick wick in the centre.

These lamps are primarily supposed to give light to the spirits of those unfortunate people who have been drowned in the lake. I found this was not entirely the fact, for if each of these lamps represented an accident, that must be the most tragic spot on earth!

The lamps are set afloat chiefly for divination on personal matters, and are intended to foretell, in some cases, the fate of those afar off at sea, and, in others, the duration of a beloved life, or the probable shortening of the life of some hated rival. At times two were floated off together—binary lamps, to ascertain if a betrothal that was being arranged would prove propitious, or whether, by the extinction of the lamp that represented the husband, his bride had a risk of being left in the much dreaded state of widowhood. A keen merchant would quietly launch one to know whether some great specu- lation in business would be successful. Whatever was the object of setting these tiny lamps afloat, they were

A CHINESE TEMPLE.

all watched with intense interest, and often with great excitement.

These floating interrogations to the Fates made a beautiful appearance as they moved hither and thither, blown about by the slight currents of wind that crept over the surface of the lake. Some blazed up with a

spurt, and then suddenly died out in darkness. Others
went away with a brilliant, steady light, floating far off,
till each lamp looked merely like the reflection of some
bright star in the dome of heaven overhead. Some
caught in the long reeds and became stationary. Others
were stopped in their course by a fibre of grass, that
would arrest the tiny lamp for a moment; then the fibre
would perchance ignite, and, burning through, set the
brilliant wanderer free to tell a false life story to some
anxious heart.

We became intensely interested in watching the
lotus lamps. Not one of the pleasure boats stirred an
oar while these indications of destiny were making their
respective voyages. At length these twinkling lights
all died out, and each questioning heart has turned
homewards with its fully believed sad or joyous answer.
We drew a long breath to shake off the spell of watching. A few strokes of the oar floated us to the steps of
the temple, where a mule was waiting for my husband,
who just arrived as the lamps were extinguished. He
had been all day engaged in the streets of the city
preaching the Gospel and selling Christian books. In
the soft moonlight we walked to our inn, revolving in
our minds that the Chinese are not so prosaic as they
are generally considered.

Early the following morning we sent our shendzles
ahead to wait for us outside the Mahommedan mosque.
As we reached the great street of the city the sun was
rising. At one of the cross streets there was a block, occa-
sioned by a train of immense wheelbarrows laden with
crockery. From a side street there emerged a sad *cortège*
—four men carrying on their shoulders an open bier, on
which a young man was laid in his last sleep. His face was

exposed ; a noble face it was, with fine features. Beside
the cold dead hand, that could never use them more, were
laid an ink-stone and a packet of books. The bearers of
the dead were obliged to press close up to where we stood.
Our guide entered into conversation with them. They
said that the young man, who died in the night, had not
been sick ; that he only gave two moans and was gone.
He was the only son of a rich family, was of great ability,
and had been in for examination. Evidently he was rich,
because the quilt that covered him was of handsome silk.
The ends also of the pillow on which his head rested were
exquisitely embroidered. The body was being borne to
the Morgue temple, there to lie till his friends should come
with a coffin for him. My mind went back to the palace
on the lake. I could not lose the idea that he was one
of the group of gay young students whom I had seen
lolling over the parapet.

> ‘ The doubly dead,
> In that he died so young.’

What hopes died out with that life we cannot tell.
I felt sorrow fill my heart for the lonely home.

This Morgue temple is indispensable, as the customs
of China prevent any one sheltering the dead. Such
temples are under the control of the district mandarin.
If a poor man dies far from home, a coffin is provided
for him by the authorities, and he is buried in the free
burial-ground ; but rich men often lie in coffins in these
temples for a long time.

Every owner of property is held responsible for the
death of any person whose corpse is found on his
premises. Hence, when any one seems near death in a
stranger’s house, he is at once carried towards his own
home. If he dies on the road, and the distance is too

great, there is always the Morgue temple where he can
be laid.   A proper-minded Chinaman cannot bear the
thought of dying in the house of a friend, as thereby he
might get his host into serious trouble.   In Scotland I
felt the shock of this difference of custom.   Some one
used the expression, 'He was a great friend of mine,
and died at my house.'   But, as a Chinaman thinks
that his greatest enemy could not serve him worse than
to die in his house, he would have said in such a case,
' The man had no manners.'

A very choice, refined, and effectual way of punish-
ing an enemy is to commit suicide on his premises.
The following instance came under my notice : A large
and handsome house was just completed, when, in
order to make the landlord suffer for some fancied
wrong, a carpenter entered one of the finest rooms,
fastened up the door, and then deliberately hanged
himself to a beam.   It was many days ere the landlord
thought of opening the door.   He believed it had been
closed to keep the beautiful pillars and other decorations from being spoiled.   Judge of his surprise when
he discovered the state of matters.   The unfortunate
landlord was hurried off to the court of justice.   He
was imprisoned, fined, and, in fact, ruined.   The house
could not be occupied by a respectable tenant.   For a
long time it was empty.   A large contingent of soldiers
arrived, and some of the officers were glad to get shelter
in the house.   Eventually it was let out piece-meal to
coolies and vagrants to whom its history was unknown.
As we walked through the street, I could not help
thinking on the strange contrariety of all things
Chinese.

In due time we reached the Mahommedan quarter

of the city, and found that the mosque was a gorgeous building. We entered by a small side door, and there, straight before us, was a broad flight of steps rising to a great height. At intervals a landing broke the ascent. The steps terminated at a large pavilion supported on handsome pillars. This pavilion formed one side of the square court in front of the great hall. The hall is approached by a flight of steps, broad and handsome, and running all along the front part of the building. The mosque had just been repaired. The paint and gilding were quite fresh, and the whole place had a look of gorgeousness not usual in Chinese buildings. The wide portico in front was decorated by many large mottoes beautifully framed. The mottoes chiefly referred to the attributes of God, and were entirely different from those that are put up in heathen temples. Indeed, these scrolls might have decorated any place of divine worship. The mottoes were: 'God, the Pure and True'; 'The Incomparable.' The great worship hall is very lofty, and the ceiling beautifully panelled and painted in fine colours, the prevailing tints being grey, green, and gold. The roof is supported on a number of massive wooden pillars lacquered in crimson. The hall is probably over two hundred and fifty feet square. The floor is covered with a very thick matting that must have been woven on the floor, as it encircles the pillars without break or seam.

I was told that only on special days were women allowed to enter. I was invited to go in, and told to take off my shoes if I did so. I did not feel inclined to enter, as I could see all that the hall contained. In it were a pulpit or two for preaching, a lectern, a number of red tables, and lacquered side tables with racks on

the back for holding candles.   The arched door into the
holy of holies was covered with Arabic characters.   A
fine Arabic scroll in gilding was over the arch.   There
were some framed mottoes, also in Arabic.   A very fine
one was over the lectern in Chinese, with again the
motto, 'The Incomparably True and Pure One.'   At
the east end was a magnificent screen of brass scroll-
work, very lofty.   The whole place was beautifully
kept, and most tasteful shrubbery adorned the garden
of the A-houn's house.

Returning from the hall of worship, I was received
by a number of fine-looking women, whose features
differed entirely from the Chinese.   They were all tall,
from five feet four to five feet eight, had finely arched
noses and abundant hair.   The hair of some of them
was quite grey, almost snow-white, a thing seldom seen
among Chinese women.   The whole pose of their figures
was noble.   The eldest amongst the group spoke much,
and claimed me as a worshipper of the true God.   We
were standing at the top of the lofty flight of steps,
whence we could see many heathen temples embowered
in the trees away off on the hillsides.   To these temples
she pointed in scorn, and said, 'These people make
with their own hands gods of clay and worship them.
We worship the true and pure One.'   As she stood
with outstretched arm and flashing eye, she might
have been a Miriam or a Deborah.

These women told me that their special duties were
teaching schools and instructing the women.   They did
not go out to teach, but they said there are always men
marrying ignorant women who need teaching, and
children growing out of babyhood to be instructed.
In the boys' schools they teach the Chinese classics.

Mahommedans take degrees and become mandarins, just as those who adhere to the other religions of China do. China is indeed very tolerant, and resents interference with politics more than interference with religion. These Mahommedan ladies very kindly invited me to take tea with them and see over their schools. They were dressed in the same dress as Chinese ladies, but had their feet the natural size.

Only one A-houn could read Arabic, and we had not taught any one else. He was the head A-houn, a fine-looking and most intelligent man, who was hoping soon to visit Mecca. Dr. Williamson presented him with copies of some of his own writings in Chinese.

With great politeness the ladies escorted us out and bade us adieu, telling us that when we returned to the city we must visit them. They were exceedingly kind, and sympathised with me over the miseries of shendzle travelling. We passed down the great flight of steps. At the door we found our shendzles waiting, and got over that stage of our journey in good time to reach our halting-place before dark.

CHAPTER XVI.

Tsi-nan-foo in Carnival time—Comical heterogeneity of the fair—A
Chinese auctioneer: his tricks of trade—The natural fountain
of Tsi-nan-foo—Encounter with a bear—Merry-makers of many
kinds—Contrast between the theatres of China and Rome—The
mosque revisited—Two heroines.

On this occasion we visited Tsi-nan-foo in the spring,
and during Carnival time. Holiday makers were
numerous. A large space around the great temple
and all its courts were completely occupied with
booths and stalls, on which goods of every description
were exposed for sale. There were stalls completely
filled with whips; stalls where pens alone were sold;
stalls for ink-stones; stalls for books—the Chinese
classics in most choice editions, and novels innumerable; stalls for shoes with the whitest of soles; stalls
for hats of most fashionable shapes; stalls filled with
toys; and stalls for sham jewellery and endless quantities of pins and other ornaments wherewith the
Chinese women decorate their hair. These last stalls
were surrounded by many purchasers, showing that
Mrs. John Chinaman is not forgotten when John goes
out for a holiday. The toy stalls were also much
patronised, and juveniles were strutting about in the
splendours of wooden swords, brilliantly painted, their
faces adorned by false moustaches of the fiercest cut.

Smaller children shook rattles, flourished whips, and hugged toy horses.

Most interesting to me was a fine pavilion, where the sale of plants was going on· quite briskly. The favourites were dwarf flowering shrubs. Many dwarf fruit trees were laden with blossoms. Small evergreen cypresses were trained and thinned into exact representations of miniature forest trees. Some of these were really beautiful, and would have been prized as table decorations in England. There were hundreds of monthly roses in various hues—deep red, pale pink, sulphur, gold colour, and pale blush. There were quantities of grafted roses ; many rose trees which would bloom during May and June; flowering plants growing in water, such as the lotus ; and various kinds of narcissus. There was a most charming display of peonies, and of the favourite flower of the Chinese artist, the *maw tan hwa*. The air around the pavilion was fragrant with the sweet scent of the *kwei hwa*. It spoke well for the taste of Tsi-nan-foo and neighbourhood that such a display of flowers was possible, and also that the prices given were very high.

In some of the larger booths outside the temple courts Cheap Jack was at work, offering his wares, and vigorously bidding against himself—beginning at fabulous prices, then suddenly coming down to the value of the article.

The street auctioneer is one of the wits of China, and a good deal of coarse buffoonery is indulged in for the benefit of the rustics. I stood outside one of the tents for a few minutes. The man was going on in a loud chant that was quite dramatic, changing his tone, as if two speakers were engaged, and when an article of woman's apparel was being offered feigning a feminine voice.

A great many gambling tables were spread about; also the tables of letter-writers, soothsayers, fortune-tellers, and various other unauthorised prophets of lucky or unlucky days.

Very few women were visible, and these elderly; but many pretty little girls were carried about by their fathers, to get a peep at all the bravery of the fair. There was a great amount of good-natured joking, and but few attempts at rude horse-play. I saw no intoxicated men, and no drinking-booths. There were innumerable peripatetic kitchens. The Chinese take a little spirit with their food, but have not the habit of drinking, so sadly prevalent in Western lands. Of course there would be opium smoking in out-of-the-way dens, but these revellers at the fair had not an opium-smoking look.

This fair is held annually. Many of the articles brought to it for sale are the results of the winter's labours of the peasants in remote villages. It is the market whence pedlars and small country shopkeepers replenish their stock. One of its great attractions is a grand theatrical display; but this year the death of the Empress Tzr Ann prevented the company from acting, and the theatre was closed. I heard many of the rustics bemoaning the consequent dulness of the fair.

As we passed in and out among the booths the people were most civil, though they followed us in crowds. We went over all the temple to the innermost shrine. In the central court is a most beautiful natural fountain, where an enormous amount of water is thrown up daily. The main gush is a foot in diameter. Many smaller gushes rise up all over the surface of the small lake

round which the temple buildings stand. From out this
basin there flows a large stream of water—in truth, a
rushing river, that supplies the lake. The water is pure
and crystalline, slightly warm, as in frosty weather, they
tell me, it 'smokes' all over. In all parts of the city
there are springs. If these were utilised for decorative
purposes, Tsi-nan-foo might be made a lovely city.

As we left the fair I tried to avoid the crowds by
turning sharply round a large stall at a corner of the
temple. I nearly ran into the paws of a great black
bear, who was standing on his hind legs. He had been
going through a number of military manœuvres, and was
for a time deserted for the rival attractions of a foreign
woman. I felt surprised when I found myself close
under the paws of the immense shaggy beast. Fortunately Bruin was occupied hugging a large brass basin.
I believe our astonishment was mutual, else he might
have visited vengeance on his rival. However, I made
a rapid retreat. I had the best of him, for he was
chained, but his chain was long enough to have enabled
him to come some few paces in pursuit.

As we get disentangled from the labyrinth of stalls
and booths we find that the ground around is much
occupied with merry-makers. The Punch and Judy
show is attracting crowds. Innumerable boys are
walking on stilts. A band of musicians, also on stilts,
make 'music in the air.' There is a general tone of
happiness all round, and a comforting odour of cooked
viands. It makes one think of Juvenal's saying about
'*panem et Circenses*.' A Chinaman must have something comfortable to eat. He is a civilised creature, a
kindly soul who never brings into his games aught that
is cruel, so that they contrast most favourably with the

I

scenes in the amphitheatres of Rome and Alexandria, where torture and death alone could amuse the populace. A Chinaman enjoys a pleasant theatrical performance, where the court of an emperor is well represented, and where the crafty knave falls into his own snare. The cold-blooded tortures and cruelties alleged against the Chinese are all under the auspices of the magistrates' offices and imperial decrees. The masses are not embruted by such spectacles as we read of in classic history. Their horrors are all confined to punishments for crime.

Passing from all the hilarity of the fair we got into some quiet streets, and thence paid a visit to our old friends at the Mahommedan mosque. We had exchanged cards, and the A-houn and his retinue were exceedingly friendly and civil; but the crowd that followed us was quite unceremonious, and rushed in, up the lofty flight of steps, and even into the private garden of the A-houn. We made our visit shorter than either the Mahommedans or we intended, as we were much afraid lest the numbers of people might spoil the fine shrubbery.

The great hall was just as we had seen it on our former visit. We had not leisure to visit the lady teachers. We learned that the head lady had died during the past year, and that our favourite A-houn had gained his wish, and was in Mecca. I scanned the crowd closely and saw that many of the faces were not Chinese. I noticed particularly that the hair was different, lighter in colour and finer. Their manners, however, were not in the least affected by this difference, as they were just the same crowding, pushing, staring throng.

I almost felt inclined to take back what I had said about the Parisian look of Tsi-nan-foo. This morning it was simply detestable. Rain had fallen during the previous day, and the streets were filthy in the extreme. The mud was so deep and sticky that I was fearful the coolies would abandon me to my fate. However, they took it as a regular part of the play, and trudged through right manfully. We came across one of the numerous runs of water, so the coolies set the sedan down, walked into the stream, washed their shoes, then their feet, and finally their faces. When these ablutions were completed, they shouldered the sedan and marched cheerfully off to the eastern part of the city.

Since the opening of the northern ports of China, in 1860, gentlemen have travelled through Shan-tung. It was not considered desirable that families should reside in the interior cities. Lately, however, since the Chinese have become accustomed to foreigners, both British and American Missions have been able to rent houses, and two families now reside in this city and several in other parts of the interior.

All honour to these missionaries and to the brave, devoted women who have chosen to uphold their husbands in the interior. It is depressing to live in a Chinese city; the houses are so closely packed together, that the only view one can have from them is the strip of sky overhead, and what variety the clouds can there give. But these ladies are happy and contented, helpful to their husbands in their work, and show to the Chinese the examples of well-ordered households.

CHAPTER XVII.

To the south-east of Tsi-nan-foo is a hilly road leading
to the most noteworthy portion of Shan-tung. We are
now in classic China, and can use a road-chart made
about twelve hundred years B.C., and a most respectable map it is. Climbing the hills to the south of
the capital, ever and anon we looked back over the
mighty city, sorry to leave its lively streets and busy
crowds. In our ten days' stay we had seen hundreds
of its women, and found them exceedingly religious.
Amongst them I found many fine, matronly women who
had for twenty or more years scarcely missed attending
the temples at the new and the full moon, the first and
the fifteenth of the Chinese months. In some of the
zenanas I found women who eagerly upheld their idols,
and even amongst themselves were emphatic on the
merits of a favourite shrine. Thus the city of Tsi-nan-

foo, with its many wealthy zenanas, had attractions in my eyes greater than almost any Chinese city I had visited, and as its lofty walls and gateways vanished from sight I hoped that ere long I might be permitted to revisit it.

We stopped at a clean little inn; and as the story of a foreign lady travelling had preceded us, the women of the place were all in holiday dress, and all on the look-out. The visit of a foreign sister was a new event in their lives, and each seemed determined to get her fair share of the show. They crowded the courtyard, and inspected me with no little interest. This interest speedily increased when I began to talk to them, and make myself known as a thorough Chinese lady. There is a sort of talismanic power in striking at once into the interests, the hopes, and the fears that make up the lives of Chinese women. At once the bond of sympathy is recognised, and question after question will follow till they begin to lose sight of the foreigner in the sympathetic woman. They took very kindly to the thought that I had come to announce a doctrine for women—a Saviour as ready to help them as to help men, and a means by which they all might attain to heaven at the last.

After quite a long talk in the courtyard, and a promise that after the sun was set I would come out and have another chat, I entered the inn, but had scarcely shaken the dust from my garments when there was a most polite invitation from one of the wealthy families that I should visit their house. This invitation was made emphatic with what in their eye is the most important reason they could urge, viz. that the old great-grandmother, who was eighty-three years of age, wished to see me, but she was not able to come.

Such is their respect for age that to refuse to gratify a request of this kind would be looked upon as an unkindness of the most heartless description. The young man who brought the invitation was fine-looking and intelligent; he had seen my husband on some former journey, and claimed us as old friends. I was glad to comply with the request, as I knew that I should have an opportunity of meeting the inmates of some of the neighbouring zenanas as well as the one to which I was invited. Of course the ladies of these zenanas could not gratify their curiosity by coming to the inn-yard.

After a short rest and a cup of tea, in the pleasant afternoon light, I made the call, and was introduced to quite a bevy of beauties. The *élite* of the village were gathered to see this foreign wonder. There were smiling young girls, dignified, silent, young Chinese wives, middle-aged, loquacious matrons, and inquisitive grand-mothers, all surrounded by a small mob of women-serv-ants and nurses with their infant charges. In the midst —queen of them all, as if holding court—was the aged Chinese great-grandmother of eighty-three.

Contrary to my experience, this lady in her old age was very beautiful. She had a clear, delicate complexion; bright, dark eyes, in which there was no sign of age; her hair was snowy white, yet still so abundant that she had no need for the head-band generally worn by the aged women. Her jacket of bright blue brocaded silk made a fine contrast to her silvery crown of hair. Altogether she looked, and I am sure she was, most lovable. For forty-two years she had ruled the household alone; this had given dignity to her deportment, and in her manner there was a peculiar graciousness.

Some most exquisite confections were served, and then tea and pipes and tobacco. We had a long, pleasant conversation, the old Tai Tai, as she was called, asking some most apt questions. While we elder women were talking the young beauties drew near, and to each other commented on my dress, my manners, the immense size of my feet, and also expressed their appreciation of the fact that my language was the same as their own.

In a pause of the conversation suddenly there was an enquiry for some one named Mae Koo, or Hawthorn Blossom. Her mother, an active-looking matron of forty or thereabouts, answered for her : ' Oh, she has been so indolent that for three months she has not made even a pair of shoes. We scolded her day after day, so now I have punished her.'

' How old is she ? ' I asked.

' Seventeen,' was the answer.

Wondering what kind of punishment she had given her daughter, and also wishing to learn a new lesson on their domestic life, I said I should so much like to see the young lady. The bevy of beauties giggled, but her mother at once said, ' Oh yes ! come; she will like to see you.' Leading the way to a suite of apartments at the extreme north of the courtyard, she lifted a silken curtain and ushered me into a pretty room, with some very finely-carved wooden figures standing on a side table. There was no sign of an occupant. The brick bedstead, or *kang*, was faced all round with about two feet of open carved work, and there in one corner stood an exceedingly beautiful young woman, tied up by her thumbs ! The silken braid with which her thumbs were fastened was so put round the offending digits, that while not hurting, it was impossible to get out, and efforts for release would only tighten the tie.   A most uncomfortable position, and quite trying enough to prevent idleness in any maiden !

There she stood, her tiny feet resting on one of the hard pillows they are so fond of using, and spread out before her a fine confusion of silk and satin scraps, half-made shoes, and unfinished embroidery, and in a tangle all sorts of tinsel and fancy braids.   These she had to gaze upon—a quiet reproach in every unfinished thread.

‘ There is Miss Idleness,’ said her mother, ‘ and there are all the things she ought long ago to have finished. How will a young lady like that ever finish a wedding trousseau, even if she begins it ? ’

‘ Now that I have come to see her you will take her down,’ I pleaded.

The girl’s pretty face was sulky, but there was a look of interest in her eyes when she heard me speak.

I said, ‘ I am sure after this you will be more diligent,’ and I quoted two lines from their woman’s classic.

The mother said, ‘ I am not going to take the trouble to clamber up and release you ; I’ll send Mae Fang.’

We departed, and Mae Fang did her duty in untying her friend ; but the idle young lady could not be induced to join the talkers in her grandmother’s sitting-room.   It would not be expected ; no one feels dignified after being punished.

In the North I have always found Chinese mothers exceedingly careful that their daughters should be trained to industrious habits.   The beautiful embroidery made in all Chinese zenanas is a great blessing to the secluded ladies.   Like the tapestries of the olden time in Western lands, in making these embroideries there is a great deal to interest the mind and exercise the

taste. Ladies draw their own patterns on the material,
and are constantly on the look-out for some new design
in this style of decorative art. In a large zenana there
are always one or two ladies who have great facility
with their pencils. In working the embroidery they
select with great care the various colours and shades.

In the Li-Ki, Book of Rites, B.C. 800, the law is laid
down for zenanas. ' From their tenth year girls are not to
be allowed to go out. A widow is to teach them tender-
ness, grace, and obedience. They are to be taught to
work in hemp and linen, to manage silk cocoons, to braid
trimmings and fringes. They are to learn all kinds of
women's work, and to make garments. They are to
learn to look after sácrifices, take charge of sauces,
pickles, fruit, and meat. In all the worship they are to
assist at offerings before the gods.

' In their fifteenth year they are to receive ornaments
for the hair, to show that they are grown up. In their
twentieth year they are to be married, unless they are
mourning for a parent. In that case in their twenty-
third year they are to be married.

' When the parents are seventy years old, the
management of the zenana is put into the hands of the
eldest son and his wife. But if the father dies before
the mother is seventy, all must submit to the old
mother.'

This zenana was well ordered and governed according to the rites. After many invitations to return and
visit them we made our adieus, escorted to the library
door by all the elder ladies, and from thence to the
inn-yard by two middle-aged waiting women.

With a feeling of regret, as though parting from
friends, I left the tidy little room and the bright faces.

I believe the pure mountain air had given them a beauty of complexion and an elasticity of spirits unusual in Chinese women.

The night was miserably cold, and before daybreak we started over a wild and rocky road. We crossed the ridge just as the sun glinted over the hills and sent a flush of gold athwart a scene very like the banks of the Tweed at Berwick, only on a grander scale. There was a stretch of lofty hills where the limestone, having decayed, had left many a pillared temple. The whole scene recalled

> ' Norham's castled steep,
> And Tweed's fair river, broad and deep.'

On the steeps on either side there were numerous *wei tzles*, or refuges, with their banks of loose stones in readiness for the pates of robbers, and far below in the valley the river lay winding through.

The bank on which the road is made is high and torn off, leaving the side abruptly precipitous down to the water, some eighteen or twenty feet below, showing that at times the stream must rush along with great violence and carry off masses of earth. There were immense numbers of beautiful ducks swimming and paddling on the shallow side of the river. There were also great flocks of geese in charge of most warlike ganders, keeping the flock together, much as collie dogs tend a flock of sheep.

These fierce birds were utilised by the farmers to keep watch in their yards, and the noise made by some of these was as effective in rousing the inmates as any ' watch-dog's honest bark ' could be. Certainly to the intruder the noise was more disagreeable, while the beat of the extended wings and the snap of the great beak were exceedingly formidable.

The country we were now traversing is the centre of classic China, where every hill has a history and monuments telling of the visits of emperors to the temples of the sages. The temples are historic, built to men famous for wisdom in all departments of life; to men whose engineering skill was called out to save the country from the floods of the Yellow River; and also to men who had guided the state through many a troublous epoch. What tributes to brain power are found all over classic China! Tablets everywhere, and once we came on a genuine pyramid, the tomb of Shao Hao, who is said to have reigned B.C. 2597–2513.[1]

We crossed the beautiful Wan river, famous for its sounding stones, and picked up pieces of coarse hourblende, which, on being struck, gave out a clear, sonorous note, the larger and thicker giving the deepest tone. These stones, it is recorded, formed part of the taxes mentioned in the *Tribute of Yü*, some two thousand two hundred years B.C.; and in the catalogue of the imperial musical instruments such stones are mentioned. They are suspended on a frame and tuned to a scale.

In this neighbourhood the villages had a most comical appearance, as roof, walls, and sometimes even the doors, were covered over with paper, drying and bleaching—a very poor paper made chiefly from straw and old rope.

In the afternoon light we descry one of the places of special pilgrimage in Shan-tung, the Tai Shan, which is the highest peak of a range of hills. Afar off we can see the temples on its summit, their brilliant red walls presenting a fine contrast to the green of the hill. We

[1] See *Journeys in North China*, vol. i. p. 234.

seem to travel round the hill, always keeping the temple in sight and not getting nearer, when suddenly, at the foot of the hill, we reached the city of Tai-ngan-foo. In the time of pilgrimages this city is very lively and interesting, being full of pilgrims, old and young, men, women, and even little children. Everything was quiet as we reached our inn, a fine large courtyard with suites of apartments dotted all over it. Our innkeeper was civil, but seemed to have a decided objection to our having anything cooked; and finally we ordered supper from a cookshop, and most palatable it was, costing as much as a supper in a first-class restaurant in England.

It was a glorious evening, so we proceeded to inspect the great temple in the city, built to the divinity of the Tai Shan, which is the chief of the five Sacred Mountains of China. The history of its worship goes back to far remote times. It is said to have been an object of worship 2255 B.C. There are authentic histories to show that for more than four thousand years generation after generation has worshipped here. People and sovereigns have alike paid homage at this hill. It seems as if each generation had had its own particular deity, sometimes a god, sometimes a goddess, just as feeling moved them. For all these generations has prayer been made here, and emperors have left records of their visits. Still the pilgrims come year by year, with only a vague idea of what benefit they are going to receive.

Over the entrance to the great temple there is a tablet, and on it is inscribed ' Tai Shan is decreed to give happiness.' Still the quest, in East and West alike, is happiness. How pathetic is all this striving for happiness ! The human heart desires that for which it was created. When will the world find it in obeying

the gracious words, ' Come unto Me, all ye that labour
and are heavy laden, and I will give you rest ' ?

The lofty gateway of the temple faces the south, and
the great street running east and west is called the
' Way or Pass to Heaven.' The entrance is a most magnificent stone arch of the kind known in China as a *pai
fang*, i.e. square at the top. This arch looks loftier
than its actual height, as there is a paved sloping walk
leading up to it. Straight in front there is a beautiful
pavilion, where, we were informed, officials who find the
emperor's business too urgent for them to take time to
ascend the mountain may worship looking towards its
summit. ' Far-off audience' this is called! Another fine
arch, and then the main gateway is reached. A row of
five immense gateways, the central one for royalty, the
others for magistrates, the outmost two for subjects ; but
one only stands open. The space within is very large,
as the wall is three and a half li round, i.e. over a mile.

The temple itself is a fine lofty building, the roof
supported on ninety pillars, some forty feet high, all
shining with pure vermilion lacquer. The whole place
is worthy of Imperial China. It would take a day to
see it and admire its galleries and temples and elaborate
imperial tablets. Nature too has done much for it, as
the cypress trees were very beautiful, as well as the
courts and walks of soft green grass. In some places
there were tables where tea was being sold, and literary
men chatting in learned fashion between their sips.

During the pilgrimage season, fairs, theatres, auctions, &c., are held in the courts of the temple.

Before sunrise the next morning two mountain chairs
were ready, and the bearers having laid in a quantity
of solid flour bread, we started for the top of the Sacred

Mountain. The hill is a veritable Pilgrim's Progress done in stone. Temples, pavilions, arbours, inscriptions, records of imperial visits made—sometimes, in adverse circumstances—bridges, grottoes, and monuments. One particularly attracted me : a great stone obelisk, and not a single character on it! We were gravely told it was erected to the emperor who burned the books, and, as a reproach to his ignorance, not a character was cut on it. Satire in earnest!

China's history is well represented here, as almost every noteworthy emperor and sage has mention, honourable or otherwise. Up and up we go, passing 5,640 steps either cut in the rock or built upon it. Many spots bear most poetical names. I am afraid to look downward as the men climb near the summit, and we come to a flat sort of bridge called ' Touch the Sky,' then to the ' Gate of Heaven.'

Here we rest, and the men point out a spot to me which is the most precipitous of all, and certainly overlooks a fearful precipice. A wall is built to prevent access to it. Many pilgrims were in the habit of making vows that if the gods of the Tai Shan spared the life of a father or a mother, they would return and cast themselves from thence, and be dashed to pieces on the rocks below—a sacrifice to the gods, as an act of filial piety. This became so frequent that government had to interdict the practice, and one of the emperors gave orders to build the wall.

A glorious view rewarded us for our long climb. A clear blue sky, not a cloud or a tint of haze. North of us hills lay, range after range in their grandeur and solitude. Southwards and eastwards and westwards stretched the great plain of Shan-tung, an ocean of grain.

We could only see the Wun river by its gleaming waters winding through, and the many brooks like silver streaks that fall into the main river. The city of Tai-ngan-foo we had just left, lying close to the hill, looks small, its great temple walls scarcely visible. In the pilgrimage season, on the day of the full moon, sometimes as many as ten thousand persons ascend the hill.

We made a rapid descent, and at times it seemed dangerous. The chair coolie tripped once, and but for the presence of mind of his neighbour, who grasped an iron chain that was fixed in the parapet, we should have been sent whirling down some thirty or forty granite steps. I could see they felt the danger by the scared look on their faces and the smothered exclamation.

By the side of a brawling stream we came down, and finally the coolies deposited me at the door of a pretty temple. Out came three or four of the occupants, each smoking a long pipe. They escorted me in after a fashion that took my companions by surprise. But the explanation was simple : the place was a nunnery, and they were nuns, dressed in every way like priests, and with large feet. 'North Pole Queen' was the name of this temple or nunnery.

They took me into a large hall, and from the back window there was a lovely peep of a cascade. A most romantic spot these nuns had chosen, and they had a most comfortable home. They were intelligent women, and gave me a graphic description of the great temple in Tai-ngan-foo, of which we have spoken. Temple after temple on the hill had fallen to decay ; but they were always rebuilt at an enormous expense. The imperial treasury was always ready with grants of money. Only recently the whole place had undergone repair.

These bright and lively nuns claimed kin with me, for had we not the same large feet, and were we not living to help our fellow-creatures? The eldest, who was a scholar, and who enjoyed the fun of my making Chinese quotations, declared that I ought to come and live with them and teach the pilgrims. They told me they got very large sums of money, and they beautified the temple with it. Rich ladies often come to stay with them during the pilgrimage time.

Parting from the nuns, we visited a priest sitting in his bones, who died a hundred and thirty years ago. He was sitting cross-legged in a shrine, where he had sat and starved himself to death in search of immortality. Far less ghastly than the friars of the chapel of St. John in Malta, yet he was not a pleasant object. Over his face is a mask, and around his shoulders a mantle. As we passed out a number of people entered and prostrated themselves before this piece of departed humanity. I believe he is a good source of revenue to the priests.

Seen from the garden of this temple, the Tai Shan presents a very remarkable sight. It would be difficult to find elsewhere a hill with so many human associations. And in a religious sense also it is a great monument, testifying to the cry of the human heart for something to worship. The Emperor Shun is said, in the first year of his reign, to have worshipped 'Heaven.' This term 'Heaven' is precisely the same as we have, when the prodigal returned. He said, 'I have sinned against Heaven': it means the Most High God. Afterwards there was worship made to the spirits of the hills and rivers. In all the temples on this hill, and upon the monuments, there is nothing that approaches the sensuous; all is pure, and this tells its own tale as to Chinese mind and feeling.

In the dim grey of early morning, we bade farewell to the city of Tai-ngan-foo, and set our faces toward the land of China's greatest sage, Confucius. Great he must have been, as no man has ever influenced so many minds; and the teachings of no other man have such amazing power over the minds of so many millions. And this power was gained by wisdom alone. Confucius never sought by any undue means to gain this influence; no pretended revelation from heaven, no tales of visions and messages in supernatural ways. In a clear and straightforward manner he expounded The Art of Living. He was wise in this—that he kept his teaching strictly to things within his knowledge. The problem of life must have been much before his mind, when he descanted on the five relations, viz. between sovereign and subject, between father and son, between elder brother and younger, between husband and wife, and between friend and friend.

It was rather a risk venturing on such classic ground as the city of Kio-foo-hien. How would the descendants of the sage tolerate a foreign woman wandering about the tomb and temple of the 'teacher of ten thousand ages'? These questions came up as we traversed the road on the banks of the Sze Shui river, another of the streams famous anterior to the time of Abraham, and spoken of in the *Tribute of Yü*, for certain articles that were sent from the neighbourhood as taxes. Near this river is the hill always associated with the mother of Confucius, on which there is a famed temple in honour of the mother of the great man.

K

It was a hot autumn afternoon when we reached the Mecca of China. Scarcely had we deposited our travelling impedimenta in a wretched inn, with a floor of clay and walls of mud and straw, when two servants from the palace arrived with a request to know the names of the illustrious travellers. My husband's card being given to the men, in about half-an-hour the messengers returned with four coolies bearing an exquisite luncheon. The duke had sent his card and a message of great kindness. On a former occasion my husband had visited the palace. The message now was that they still had a pleasant remembrance of his visit; would so like to see him again, but, alas! the shadow of death was hovering over the palace : the beloved mother had but a few hours to live, the whole place was in sorrow, and the grave-clothes were being prepared.

Although the palace was in the utmost confusion, they would have the pleasure of receiving us in the ' hall of preaching ' within the temple; and the ladies of the family would wait on me. The doors of the temple would be thrown open to us.

The duke's card and the message were suitably acknowledged, and we promised to accept the invitation to the *kiang shu tang*, or ' hall of preaching.'

We set out to look at the city, not a very large one, but lively and busy. Our inn was close to the south gate. We found that besides the ordinary city gate to the south, there was a special gate reserved for royalty —an imperial south gate—directly in front of the celebrated Confucian temple and the street leading in a direct line to the temple gates. The west part of the city is almost entirely taken up by this temple and grounds; and in this district, it is said, Confucius lived.

It was a lesson in history to talk with the men of the place, who counted seventy-nine generations direct from the sage ; men whose ancestors in one unbroken line have lived and died in this city. More strange still is it to notice that these men, in face and figure, bear a distinct resemblance to the portrait that the old graven stones still keep in trust as a likeness of Confucius.

One tall, portly man, thirty-two years of age, interested us particularly, since he looked, I feel sure, exactly like what Confucius must have been at his age. A plausible, genial man, he seemed, obliging and likely to get on well with those in whose company he was thrown. He told us that nowadays not many of the name took high degrees in literature, feeling evidently that the fame of their great sire was quite enough for them to the end of time. When we passed his house—which was humble enough, though he was handsome and lordly—he rushed in and brought out two of his boys and their mother to see the foreigners. I gave them some foreign articles I had in my reticule, and they were greatly pleased. One thing was carefully examined and praised, a reel of J. and P. Coats's white thread ! The woman said that for many years it would suffice for stitching the black velvet ornaments on her husband's shoes.

Next day in the pleasant dewy morning we set out —according to arrangement—to visit the great temple. It stands to the west of the great gate, and there, under a verandah, were assembled quite a crowd of ladies with their attendants. Two of the elderly ladies of the family and four attendants, who also were related to the duke's household, came at once across to meet me and escort me over the temple. We had a pleasant morning. I found them most companionable and intelligent. We talked of many matters of Chinese interest, and they questioned me on many things relating to England. Queen Victoria was a favourite subject.

' What size are her feet ? ' was the first question.

' I believe about the size of the feet of the present Empress of China,' was my reply.

' Oh yes ! the Great Illustrious Empress has large feet. She is a Manchu.'

They were most anxious that I should see everything that was noteworthy. They told me that they often sat in the portion of the palace where the classics of Confucius were dug out of the walls, in which scholars had hidden them, to save them from the emperor who burned the books ; 'and of course,' said they, ' that ignorant emperor searched most carefully in the birthplace of Confucius for the classics.'

It was a new idea to them when I told them that Queen Victoria wrote books.

The part of the temple where the musical instruments are kept had great attractions for them ; and one of the younger women made a very good attempt on a kind of harp to accompany herself while she sang a favourite song, 'The mo lee wha,'—'The jessamine flower.'

We set out to view the temple. The lofty, yellow-tiled roof of the great shrine looked like gold in the sun's rays, and the marble pillars with the exquisitely carved dragons coiled at the top were a sight of beauty. The building was most carefully kept, and all round the eaves there were wire guards to keep out the birds. They were extremely proud of the shrine, and asked me

to admire the gorgeous silken curtains that covered it.
The likeness of Confucius within is a large one, eighteen
Chinese feet high, and coloured life-like. The important
part, however, to them was the *pai wai*, or worship
tablet, his spirit's resting-place.

At last we came to the preaching-hall, and there
we were served with an elegant repast, their morning
meal. Refreshing tea, cakes of many kinds, confections and some most delicious sweets with white icing,
each cake bearing the Chinese character of the duke's
name in vermilion.

Tiffin over, we were shown a temple to the father,
and another to the mother of the sage, and also, behind
all, a temple in honour of his wife.

The ladies made me promise that if there was any
amendment in the symptoms of the sick lady I would
gratify the ladies of the palace by visiting them. We
bade each other farewell, and they were quite affectionate.
In the evening many boxes of sweetmeats were sent for
our use on the road, an attention never omitted where
there is friendliness and good will. The duke's card
accompanied the present, and a message that the sick-
ness was unto death, and no hope was entertained of
the patient surviving till the morning.

In the afternoon a mounted escort was waiting to
conduct us over the graveyard. The fine avenue of
cypress trees leads straight from the north gate. The
burial-ground is of great extent, but the part where the
tomb of Confucius stands is enclosed by a high wall.
Around the grave there are some fine old trees and
beautiful shrubs. There also are the graves of his family.

We were shown the spot where his disciples built
huts and dwelt in them, mourning their master for three

years; and one favourite disciple sat for six years over his grave and mourned him. The graves of his clan are scattered over a vast extent of ground, and the enclosure contains much ground still unoccupied. The stones all bear the date of so many generations after Confucius. We saw the seventy-sixth, and were told that the young children playing round the place were the seventy-ninth generation.

CHAPTER XVIII.

TSOW HIEN, our next stage, is a city with all the most pleasing characteristics of a Chinese landscape. The exquisite pagoda, the fine old grey walls, and the picturesque range of hills lying beyond the city, make a picture so completely Chinese as to satisfy the most ardent worshipper of all that is pleasant in the peculiar style of the Flowery Kingdom. In the range of hills lying behind Tsow Hien there is one mountain of historic fame, the loftiest of the range, a high peak seen from a great distance, called the Yih Mountain. In the well-known *Tribute of Yü* this mountain is spoken of as the part from whence was brought in tribute to the emperor the wood of a famous dryandra tree, celebrated for the purpose of making lutes for the imperial palace.

At the present day this hill still has attractions for the traveller on account of the stones that take the forms of so many different things. One rock is said to be exactly like a drum, another like a bell. We did not explore the hill and its wonders, but pushed on to the southern suburb.

I had a personal interest in wishing to visit the Temple of Mencius, which is situated in this town

Through all my residence in China I had constantly heard of Meng Mu, the mother of Mencius. Her fame is in every household, and she is constantly quoted as an incentive to young mothers to take care of their children ; and constantly held up as an example of how careful mothers ought to be in regard to what they allow their children to see or become familiar with in their youthful years. Women who know nothing of what Mencius taught, know a great deal about what his mother taught him.

The Chinese idea of maternal wisdom is summed up in Meng Mu. Her boy was but an infant when his father died, leaving her residing near a large public graveyard. This she believed to be a bad surrounding for her boy, so she changed her abode. However, she had not been sufficiently careful, because she found herself in the neighbourhood of a market, and lo! a butcher opened a shop close to her house. Her boy, clever and imitative, began to watch and imitate the butcher; so, fearing this might develop a cruel nature in him, again she changed her abode, and found congenial neighbours in an adjoining school. No doubt she had some anxiety here also, as the pupils would be likely to teach the well-guarded boy not a few schoolboy tricks. At all events he was apt to be idle at his lessons and inclined to play truant. History tells us that she was obliged to resort to a most graphic object-lesson to teach the incipient sage the value of continued exertion in acquiring learning. She was engaged in weaving a web of cloth, so she cut the threads across with a knife, to show him the dangers arising from a lack of continuity. The web was a web no more, only a small piece of woven cloth and a tangle of useless thread. We can judge that the object-lesson was not lost on young Meng Ko, as his after fame amply compensated his mother for her spoiled web and her many changes of abode.

The gatekeeper recognised my husband, and at once admitted us. He congratulated me on being the wife of a sage, and laughed outright when with a touch of sadness in my voice, I informed him 'it was only the mothers of sages who were famous.'

Here, as at the Temple of Confucius, the man was anxious that we should see the whole of the wonders of the place. The most striking object to be seen on entering is a colossal tortoise of marble, bearing on his back a huge tablet. The tablet is over twenty feet high and six broad, a magnificent slab of greyish pink marble. This tablet was erected by the Emperor Kang-hi, in honour of the sage. It had a regal look. The tortoise is finely cut in black marble, and is over twelve feet long. It must have been a work of engineering skill to poise that slab on the back of the tortoise.

An avenue of cypress trees leads to the temple, and on each side stand numerous tablets in honour of the sage. Each dynasty seems to have done honour to the great man. In the main temple, which does not compare with the Temple of Confucius, there is a large statue of Mencius. It stands on a raised platform enclosed in a shrine gorgeous with carving and gilding. The statue is reported to be a good likeness, and certainly from the stone there gleams a look of power, if not of genius. With all the drawbacks of the rude skill of the graver, we can at once see that no ordinary or commonplace Chinaman is represented here. He was a man evidently of swift thought and rapid action. A Chinese face with a history. Mencius was contemporary with Plato, Aristotle, and Demosthenes. Born B.C. 371, he died at the age of eighty-four. His descendants still live here. The eldest of the present generation is seventy-two, his sons and grandsons are bright, intelligent young men. I was told that there were a few children of the seventy-third generation living at the family house.

Like Confucius, the sage Mencius taught The Art of Living, and most stoutly denounced the sins of the age. His teachings on public and private morality are weighty.

On our way home we visited the burial-ground of the family of Mencius. It lies about six miles from the city, on the southern slope of a beautiful hill. Nearing it we enter a fine avenue of cypress and yew trees. Traversing this, we come to a tablet, on which is engraved, ' Erected in honour of the holy Sage Mencius,' and on the left of this tablet is a small mountain, under which his remains repose. His mother's tomb lies on a similar hillside about eight miles distant.

CHAPTER XIX.

China's Sorrow '—Crossing the Yellow River—The ferry : ferrymen
and mules—Rural life—A fine inn, but a bad landlord—Uni-
formity of the scenery—Wheelbarrows with sails—Arid soil—
How the natives treated the gods to cause them to send rain.

WE now resume our journey to Peking along the old
highways. Four hours from Tsi-nan-foo we reached
the famous Yellow River, well called ' China's Sorrow.'
The Emperor Kia King, A.D. 1796–1811, in his will
gave it this name, and speaks of it as having been from
remotest ages ' China's Sorrow.' When we crossed it
looked peaceful enough, for the waters were low, but
the current was very rapid, and altogether it looked the
kind of stream one would not like to trust. At this
ferry there was visible one of the numerous griefs inflicted
on the government by this treacherous river, viz. a fine
bridge almost completely destroyed. In the centre of
the stream several arches still remained. Originally the
bridge seemed to have been strongly and solidly built,
but the arches had been too low. The river swept
under as long as it could, but when the waters rose and
it gained force it rushed over and carried away a great
part of the bridge.

In the hamlet above the ferry there seemed as
choice a collection of ruffians as I have ever seen. They
just matched the river—wild and turbulent they were,

evil-looking also. Our shendzles were seized by them, and they were determined to have our patronage for the night. The muleteers agreed with the fellows who wished to detain us, and with quite an effort we got to the river side. The sun was still high, and to make our proper halting-places it was necessary to cross the Yellow River that afternoon.

A large boat lay at the ferry, and the boatmen were as anxious to carry us across as the innkeepers were to detain us. So we pitted one set of ruffians against another. My husband's ideas coincided with those of the ferrymen, and we resolved to cross. The mules were unloaded, very reluctantly by the muleteers, very heartily by the ferrymen: the baulked innkeepers hovering gloomily around. The great ferry-boat already contained two immense wheelbarrows laden with delf teapots. These barrows were wheeled to the stern, and with much noise and shouting our shendzles were put on board. On the margin there was a lively scene. The mules, held firmly by the bridles, were plunging about wildly and rearing. The innkeepers stood halloo-ing, still more to exasperate the frightened animals.

But at last all are on board, and we are shoved off. We sail softly down the stream, the men managing the huge sail admirably. On the east side the current ran strongly, but on the west it was much slower. After running down with the current we tacked, and came slowly up the west bank, and disembarked at a point only a little lower down than where we had started. There was no difficulty in disembarking; the mules were soon laden, and the shendzles were just in motion, when suddenly there arose a great howl for bucksheesh. My shendzle was surrounded. A cry of disappointment arose, for the shendzle was empty, as I preferred to walk up the bank. Pell-mell they rush on my husband's shendzle. They seem as if going to devour him, mules and all. He scatters some cash, and in the scramble the shendzle escapes, and we pass on our way unmolested.

It is a lovely evening, the sun is still an hour from setting. Everything is quiet except the tinkle-tinkle of the mule bells and the lowing of oxen as they go home from the fields. One set were just ahead of us, three fine oxen abreast, and a mean little donkey with his long traces as slack as they could possibly be, not to entangle his heels. They were dragging a sledge that is used to mark the width of the furrows, with a box for sowing the seed in front. On the sledge are now piled a harrow and a plough, with its polished share brightly gleaming in the setting sun. The man behind is carrying a windlass and close basket bucket for raising water. The Chinese never leave any of their farming implements in the fields. Though their lives are primitive, their simplicity is not primitive. Neighbour does not as a rule steal from neighbour, but passing travellers consider the villagers fair prey.

Sometimes, as on this occasion, we see fine bits of real rural life. A fine mule was dragging home a small stone roller ; on his back was seated a sturdy little three-year-old boy, chubby and rosy as any farmhouse pet in either 'Merrie England,' or 'Bonnie Scotland'; a troop of larger children were following and gambolling around him. Young China was held on by his father. At the door of the house stood a smiling woman, young and pretty, clapping her hands, and holding them out for the little rider, who was kicking his little heels and crowing back to her. It was a lovely picture. The colouring also was fine ; the soft grey of the mule, the little boy with scarlet jacket and vivid green trousers, and the elder children in various shades of blue. The handsome young father also was a genuine son of the soil, burnt and copper-coloured.

Soon after crossing the Yellow River we stopped to enquire the way, and the answer to our enquiry was, ' Wang pei kii,' that is, ' Go to the north.' We went northwards. The country looked lovely in the twilight. I walked for miles along the level road, shaded at intervals by lofty elm, beech, poplar, and willow trees. At this season these have their fairest, freshest look. The wheat though short was not parched, as a shower of rain had fallen during the previous day. It was long after dark when we reached the town of Ma Kia Tien, but we found a fine inn, a Koong Kwan.

In the morning the landlord was very hard to satisfy. We got in so late that there had been no time to make an agreement as to money ; and for the honour of entertaining us with the comforts of a large wooden bench as a bed, and a little hot water for tea, he wanted the same sum that the Foo Tai [1] had paid, who had brought something like fifty followers. We could not reduce him to a reasonable charge, but compromised for about half the sum he demanded.

We now reached a part of the province where streets, shops, inns, temples have a uniform colour, and that is the colour of their fields. The people also are grim and grey-looking. ' And Adam was made out of the dust of the ground.' These words are constantly coming up to me. The walls and roofs of the houses are only stalks

[1] Governor of the Province.

of millet plastered over. Few of the houses have even
the variety of a ridge pole, or any indication of where
the one side of the roof slopes off from the other. All
is one plaster of mud. Truly 'mother earth' is *mother
earth* to them. But, with this glorious brightness of
sky, and the lovely trees, some of them all aglow with
fruit-blossoms, not even a clay-coloured village can look
quite repulsive : and ever and anon from the most
wretched hovels will peep the sunny faces of children.
Their bright blue jackets form a pleasant contrast to
the neutral tint of these sepia hamlets, as I called them,
and as one after another of these little black-eyed faces
smiled at me I could not help thinking of Dr. Charles
Mackay's lines :—

> ' Who bids for these little children ?
> Body and soul and brain.
> Who bids for these little children ?
> Young and without a stain.'

Occasionally we are startled. A distant curve of the
road seems suddenly full of sails, just like a small fleet
of pleasure boats. Each tiny sail has its ropes all taut.
Sometimes, if the wind is high, a reef is taken up in the
sail. Surely this is Liliput, and we are on the track of
elves or fairies. Such miniature sails could not propel
aught but a fairy bark. Certainly these are going
steadily and at a good rate. ' Is there water there ? ' is
a question we ask ourselves. Possibly there may be,
for low banks prevent our seeing aught; but the Lili-
putian sails are gliding on. There is a break in the
embankment, and one by one the sails fleet past the
opening. These are the land yachts of North China!
the prosaic wheelbarrows ! The sails must be of much
assistance in propelling them, for they are very heavy,

and there are generally two men, but sometimes only one, handling each wheelbarrow. Human labour could scarcely exceed the strain these wheelbarrow men bear. Milton speaks of Cathay, where Chinese 'drive their cany waggons light.' Had he seen them, and not merely

the tale in Marco Polo, he would have had to use a different adjective. Our mules don't like the sails, and are always troublesome while passing them.

We had a hot, dusty ride between Yen Tien and Ur Shih le poo. All along the way, one is almost op-

pressed by realising the great efforts required to trans-
port things from place to place. Surely the Via Victoria
ought to be here, to relieve this dreadful pressure, and
give human beings a chance of being something else
than mere beasts of burden. In the Southern provinces,
where water-ways are abundant, the urgent need of
railways is not felt, but in the North, where there are
no water-ways, railways are necessary for the well-being
of the people, to set them free from this drudgery. Had
they water-ways, these would be of no use in winter,
for this is a most tantalising climate. Neither cold
enough to freeze the rivers thoroughly, nor warm enough
to keep them thawed.

So arid it was between Ur Shih le poo, and Whang
ho Yeh that I was reminded of the alkaline plains
on the South Pacific Railway in America. The dust
brought the same biting, stinging sensation to one's eyes
and finger-nails. Yet the trees are as lovely as possible.
The frost has locked up the moisture in the soil, and
trees, striking their roots deep, flourish. The surface
looked dry, so dry, the wheat poor, and struggling hard
to live. In this neighbourhood the drought has been
trying. After praying in vain to the gods for rain,
the inhabitants at one village took down one of the
walls of a temple, so that the gods might see for themselves the dryness of the soil, and feel the glare of the
noonday sun. The people told me it was quite effectual, as on the succeeding night a good shower of rain
fell, accompanied with thunder. In the districts where
there had been no lack of rain, and the wheat was
young and green, the whole plain had a park-like look,
owing to the great number and variety of the clumps of
trees planted over graveyards.

L

CHAPTER XX.

Chinese burial-grounds—An imperial courier—Temples : the beauty
   of their sites—Chinese Christians—The spread of Christianity
   in Shan-tung—The telegraph—Whang ho Yeh—The emporium
   of Teh Chow—A great depôt on the Grand Canal—Fine *pei-low*—
   Great display of lethal weapons at every gate—Bookselling—
   Chinese 'exquisites' and Chinese roughs—Hunt for an inn—A
   guest-room tastefully ornamented—'The seven ages of man'—
   Chinese honesty.

THE Chinese government forbids intra-mural interment.
Public burial-grounds, given by government, are only
used for the very poor, or for strangers dying far away
from their homes, and who have not had money enough
to carry them to their native places. Sometimes at
the seaports, or other great places of trade, the men
from some distant province will subscribe and purchase a cemetery, where those who are rich have temporary sepulture, and the poor lie till the angel shall
proclaim that time shall be no more. Usually each
family has its own little graveyard in its own piece of
ground. Graveyards are therefore dotted over every
plain. Some of them have very fine trees. It is quite
unusual to see graves unshaded by the dark yew, or
the feathery arbor vitæ.

We have now reached the great main highway to
Peking. To-day we meet a courier with the imperial
mail for the South. A most imposing personage he

seems. His yellow silk sash, and his despatches rolled in yellow silk and tied across his shoulders, proclaim his dignity. Couriers travel very rapidly. At each stage a man waits, ready mounted, to receive the packages, and transfer them to the next stage. No delay is permitted. How interesting it would be to know what this messenger carried! Promotion to the fortunate, degradation and often decapitation to the unfortunate, for here, as in Western lands, ' nothing succeeds like success.'

We dined at a small place called Woo-li poo, or ' Five Mile Cairn.' It was a miserable little place, so wretched indeed that there was no room fit to eat in. So we had to betake ourselves to the open air. The people were kindly and polite, and it was pleasant to have the blue sky overhead.

Just after our meal an intelligent-looking man came up and saluted my husband as ' pastor,' rather a novel salutation, but a most welcome one in these parts. Of course that at once told us he was a Christian, and not ashamed of his creed. We may think that the prestige of a Briton is high, but that of a Christian is higher. A Chinaman is not at all times anxious to claim his acquaintance with a foreigner. Not unfrequently it brings down upon him many petty annoyances from his neighbours. Even the mandarins sometimes oppress those known to be friendly to the outside barbarian. This man, however, came with the utmost frankness. He told us there were a few Christians in the neighbourhood belonging to the mission of the American Board of Foreign Missions.

When my husband passed through this region in 1865, there was not a Protestant Christian nor a mission station in any part of Shan-tung, except at the ports of Chefoo and Tung-chow-foo. What a change! According to late statistics, there are now over 2,800 professed converts in Shan-tung alone, six ordained native ministers, and little groups of Christians dotted all over the province. Each year there has been an increasing ratio of baptisms. We trust this will continue: for not only does Christianity bring to Chinese hearts the joy and the healing of salvation by faith in Jesus Christ, but the advancement of Christian missions means prosperity, deliverance from superstitious bondage, and the removal of Chinese exclusiveness in every shape and form.

Near this point the telegraph line between Tien-tsin and Shanghai passes. There is now telegraphic communication from Tien-tsin, which is the port of Peking, to Shanghai, and from thence to London and all the world.[1] This has been brought about by the power and wisdom of the well-known Chinese general, Li Hung Chang, at the instigation and with the able assistance of Sir Robert Hart, the Inspector-general of the Chinese Imperial Customs. The construction of this telegraph marks a wonderful era in the history of the Chinese Empire. The Chinese have gone at one sweep from travelling couriers to telegrams, without waiting for the intermediate penny postage. Who, after this, can say that they are *slow* to adopt improvements? The successful planting and opening of this line of telegraph has been greatly aided by the amount of intelligence that has of late been spread amongst the officials and people. The distribution of books and the circulation

---

[1] A high mandarin told me lately that neither imperial mandate nor guards of soldiers would have enabled the telegraph to be erected had it not been for the information diffused by the missionaries among the people.

of periodical literature have enabled them to understand the value and utility of our Western discoveries. The frequent journeys of foreigners throughout these Northern provinces have also helped to enlighten the common people.

Very likely, in a short time, the Chinese will make a corresponding leap from ruts to railways, without going through the transition stage of macadamised roads. Chinese roads will be repaired when Chinese gentlemen require wheeled carriages to catch the trains, and waggons to bring their goods to railway depôts in time to reach stated markets. In this empire railways cannot lag far behind telegraphs ; for from speedy information will arise the necessity of speedy transit.

The city of Whang ho Yeh, meaning 'The shore of the Yellow River,' is now a very long way from that erratic stream. It has fine, lofty, arched gateways, with beautiful temples over them, though there is nothing to protect but mud inside the walls. It is astonishing how the people contrive to have some piece of beauty in these mud-built towns. The temple usually absorbs all the æsthetic powers of the inhabitants ; for although there is not a brick or a tile in the houses, they seem to get bricks, and tiles, and paint to decorate the village shrine. Care and money are evidently bestowed on their little temples, which are always built on the loveliest sites. Some of the finest trees are found in the temple grounds. I speak of small village temples. In large places the temples are often in a state of ruin and decay.

We next reached Teh Chow, a most prosperous city, the depôt for the trade by canal. The streets are wide. The shops and warehouses looked thriving. In the

centre of the city is a fine *pei-low* built of wood, the
first wooden *pei-low* we met.   The fretwork on the top
is particularly fine, with nothing of the grotesque.   At
every gate and barrier—and these were more numerous
than usual in Chinese cities—there was a grand display
of swords, spears, battle-axes, bows and arrows, javelins,
gingalls, &c.   These, however, were only painted.   The
actual weapons were in the citadel beyond—quite an
imposing structure.   They would have been formidable
in the hands of such braves as we saw loitering about.

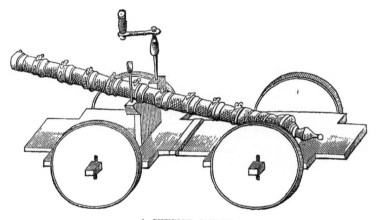

A CHINESE CANNON.

In the busiest part of the city we halted.   Dr.
Williamson took a great quantity of Testaments and
other books for sale.   While this was being done, I
watched the sour looks of the grandees in the crowd.
Fancy to yourself an 'exquisite,' tall and elegant, got
up in a long robe of sea-green brocaded crape, a violet
carmine satin jacket, a blue velvet collar, a black satin
hat with crimson tassel, irreproachably white stockings,
lavender silk shoes with black velvet toes, rubbing

shoulders with some of the most loathsome and wretched specimens of humanity I have ever seen—and there were scores of such among them, all the roughs of a most turbulent city—yet such 'exquisites' braving all this, merely to get sight of a foreign woman.

This particular dandy tried to treat me to his most elaborate sneer. While he stood at one side I looked steadily at the other, and made myself appear unaware of his presence to such an unlimited extent that he became angry. To another 'exquisite,' in a stone-coloured silk robe, a black satin sleeveless jacket, and black velvet boots, he remarked, 'What an abominable odour these foreigners have! faugh, the whole street is full of it!' Then Mr. Sea-green Robe stood right in front of the mule, and stared hard into the shendzle. Still was I imperturbable, quite regardless of his sneers and cynical remarks. The dandies then commented on my appearance, which was not to their taste. Mr. Grey Robe said, 'Think of an old man like that bringing his daughter out; these barbarians sometimes don't let their daughters marry till they are over thirty.' Mr. Sea-green questioned me :—

'How old are you?'

Mr. Grey said, 'She does not understand a word you say.'

'Oh! doesn't she though? She speaks as good Chinese as you do!' said a cheeky lad.

When they discovered I was not to be worried, they walked off to the greater attraction of the bookselling, where doubtless they harassed my husband not a little.

He was very much distracted by just such fellows as I have described. Of course, when common roughs get the countenance of the upper classes, they are apt to become very much more boisterous than they would otherwise be.

At the close of his sales that evening, Dr. Williamson tells me, a gentleman answering the description of Mr. Grey Robe, made a raid on the colporteur's basket. Snatching a handful of small books, he scattered them amongst the crowd for a scramble and made off; but not soon enough, for Dr. W. seized him by his queue; he screamed out. Dr. W. allowed him to go, as there was no credit in provoking a fight. Such conduct is a disgrace to Chinese gentlemen, especially men getting towards forty years of age.

The books were sold as rapidly as the money could be collected—Scriptures of the National Bible Society of Scotland, and books from the Religious Tract Society in London. There was very great eagerness to get both Scriptures and books. The Testaments sold were of a new edition, with maps, introductions to each book, and headings to the chapters, such as we have in our English Bibles. The Tract Society's books were a fine collection, more extensive, and better suited to the Chinese than we ever previously had. Amongst them were many periodicals like the 'Leisure Hour' and 'Sunday at Home,' mostly well illustrated. These were in great demand, also a book called the 'Two Friends,' being a story in dialogue between two China-men, illustrating the various points of our religion, and a large sheet calendar with appropriate religious texts and several illustrations.

Usually, when a man or boy became the proud possessor of a book or calendar, there was a rush to read it; and over shoulders and on all sides numbers of voices screamed out as much of its contents as they could see. Then it was pronounced *haw*, good, and a pell-mell sale was the result.

At various points Dr. Williamson made arrangements for supplying the magistrates with a copy of the 'Globe Magazine' for one year. This is a gift from the Religious Tract Society of London. The mandarins expressed their thanks for the kindness, and sent their cards. The 'Globe Magazine' is like the 'Leisure Hour,' with a few pages of news of the world.

While the bookselling was going on, the cavalcade went off to hunt up an inn, where we might stay the night. In that part of the city to which we had been directed, viz. the western suburbs, there were only wheelbarrow inns, with no accommodation for animals. So, after much questioning and going round outside the walls, we were at length directed to a very good place. The crowd that followed us in a great human tide rolled into the inn-yard. I got into the shelter of the large room of the inn. The crowd filled the courtyard and began peering in at the windows and to tear the paper. It was only with great difficulty that I forced myself from the unwelcome attentions of the gazing crowd. Left in peace at last, I found that the large room of this inn was in a Chinese fashion rather tastefully decorated. Over the sideboard, and opposite the door, was a picture quite Shakespearian. The 'seven ages of man' were painted on a long scroll such as the Chinese admire. There was age prattling to infancy, the infant held in the arms of middle age; manhood sat on a throne with an aureole of peacock feathers; youth stood slightly behind, as if attending on manhood; while boyhood and childhood were in front in the act of presenting flowers and fruit to age

and infancy.   This was a copy of a very old and favourite
picture.   It was probably an inspiration of genius before
the Bard of Avon penned his immortal lines in ' As You
Like It.'   This picture was very vivid.   It had been
recently put up, and had probably some connection
with a death in the landlord's family, as it was flanked
on either side by commemorative scrolls that told of
the ' five lakes ' and the ' four seas,' and of human life
slipping away like rivers to the ocean.   There were
drawings on crimson paper quite artistic, studies of
plants, in which the bamboo figured gracefully.   These
were all quite pleasing to my eye, and suggested the
sunny South, with its groves of fairy bamboos.   Outside,
on the whitewashed walls of the courtyard, were two
pictures in colour-wash.   On one side travellers were
represented under a lofty pine tree, on the other side
a weeping willow shaded the wayfarers.   These were
roughly done, but had the artistic touch that is so
unmistakable.

While I was admiring this picture gallery, a man
arrived with an oral message from my husband : ' The
books are nearly sold out, send more, also calendars.'

' Did the teacher not give you a paper ? '

' No ; nothing, only said, " Bring books." '

' Did he pay you ? '

' No ; but when I go back I am to have two books
for my trouble.'

The man had an honest face, though he was poor
and dirty.   I committed to his care about fifty Gospels,
fifty ' Three Character Classics,' and two hundred
calendars.   After he started I was rather doubtful of
the wisdom of the transaction ; but when a Chinaman
is *entrusted* with anything he is usually faithful.   I

was delighted to find that he conveyed all the books most faithfully ; though he was only sent hoping he would reach the inn before the colporteur started, and thus go along in his charge.

The man got the promised two books that were to recompense him for his trouble, and was as proud of his act of service as if an honour had been conferred on him.

CHAPTER XXI.

JUST outside the town of Teh Chow we crossed the celebrated Grand Canal, the direct water-way to Tientsin and Peking, and entered the province of Chih-li. There were many boats in the stream. The ferry-boat was large, and had no sail. It was simply drawn across by means of a rope, though the deep canal is at this point much wider than the Suez Canal.

About a mile distant, on the Peking side, we saw a new fort bristling with brass cannon. No soldiers were loitering about, as it was very early in the morning. At a little distance from the fort a courier on horseback overtook and passed us. His despatches were more bulky than usual, but they were covered with the genuine imperial yellow. Immediately behind him, on a beautiful black pony, rode an armed officer, to guard the precious papers. A heavy shower of rain fell, and we left them behind. Very soon they overtook and again passed us. They had stopped to cover up the packet of despatches with oilskin, and the officer had drawn an oilskin hood over his helmet. Both were pleasant-looking men. The officer remarked to the muleteer as he passed, 'How can the lady bear the cold and rain?' I could not help admiring their steeds as they galloped off. Not the usual podgy animals that mandarins delight to see, but fiery little barbs, with an Arab look about them.

In this neighbourhood are many camps of soldiers. They are towards Tien-tsin, along the line of this canal. Each camp contains five hundred men. A few of these are cavalry, but the greater portion of them are infantry. These camps are placed for the protection of the telegraph from Tien-tsin to Shanghai, of which we have formerly spoken.

At noon of this day we reached the city of King chow, a most dilapidated and poverty-stricken-looking place. The gates are imposing. Within the walls is quite a handsome pagoda. The inhabitants are few, and their houses are clustered together at the cross of the city. Their manners are rude, insolent, and almost savage. The inn where our dinner was prepared, whilst my husband went to the streets to sell books, was the only respectable-looking house in the place. It was kept by a cheery old Peking man, who complained that 'these steamers from Tien-tsin to Shanghai had taken all the trade from the interior; that formerly the traffic on this road was tremendous, but now, alas! the people here were too poor to live.' His inn was much in decay, but he pointed triumphantly to the relics of former grandeur in the fine mahogany lampstands he used to set out when illustrious guests came. He pointed to the fine tables and other furniture that had evidently been the pride of his heart. I amused him a little by declaring that I was unfortunate not to have arrived in the evening, when he might have displayed his lampstands for such an illustrious guest as a foreign lady.

In the afternoon we passed a newly dug canal, where a number of soldiers were busy driving piles for a bridge. They had erected an immensely high trestle

A CHINESE OFFICER.

scaffolding, which would have been a credit to any trestle bridge railway contractor in America. This scaffolding was to enable them to drive the piles. Probably, under each large pile would be put a living child—under the piles on the west, boys; under those on the east, girls. Alas! that men with brain enough to plan and execute engineering works of great magnitude were yet so dark with superstition as to believe that the bridge would have small chance to stand unless supported by this sacrifice of human life! Near Chefoo, we knew of eight children being so sacrificed. A wooden bridge had been frequently swept away by the turbulent stream, so that, to appease the spirit of the river, this sacrifice was thought necessary. The families from which the children were taken were poor. Each family got a handsome douceur, and the affair was

CHINESE SOLDIERS AND TENT.
(*From a Chinese drawing.*)

quietly managed. I am only sorry to add that the bridge, being constructed of heavier timbers, stands still, and the people are satisfied that they have done right. Children so sacrificed are supposed to enjoy entire freedom from punishment in after life; and the sacrifice of them is considered a meritorious act on the part of their parents, so that there is no need to mourn. Afterwards, when telling the number of their children, they never count the little ones who perished thus.[1]

[1] This I have on Chinese authority.

At the town close by the canal we could not get rooms. The place was full of soldiers and navvies. The present Board of Works are making a great effort to drain this portion of the country, which had been seriously inundated by the Yellow River some years ago. They are opening outlets that have been closed for years, and at this point are digging an entirely new canal, to open up water communication with the West and South. At one place, so many coolies were carrying round basketsful of mud that the plain resembled an ant-hill. We were told that seventy thousand men were engaged on this work, and I believe it to be the fact. No wonder the people dread these inundations. A few weeks before our visit the Yellow River overflowed at Chi Ho, the place where we crossed after leaving Tsi-nan-foo, and there has been dreadful suffering and loss of life.

Well! His Imperial Majesty's workmen obliged us to plod on for six miles, in a beating rainstorm, till we reached a much more picturesque place, called Shen Kia Lin, or, 'The Forest of the Shen Family.' That night, probably in consequence of the wetting, my husband became seriously ill. We had a small stock of medicines with us, and fortunately just what was required to check the disorder. On Saturday it rained in torrents, to the great joy of the people, for the rain saved their crops. I joined in their feelings, as my husband was improving. Next morning he was much stronger.

Sunday morning was bright and fair. About noon there came sweeping into the inn-yard, in fine style, a goodly cavalcade, shouting and flourishing.

The masters of the carts were young men; some of whom were tall, stout, and loud-voiced. In an instant

the inn-yard was completely crowded with pedlars of all
sorts of small wares. Each pedlar rattled most vigorously
a bamboo about a foot long, filled with sticks, about the
thickness of an ordinary lead pencil, and the end of the
bamboo was fitted with something that sounded like a
drum. What could all these noises mean ? The bamboos
were lottery boxes. The sticks in them were all marked
so many blanks to so many prizes. The sticks were
well shaken up and down on this resounding tym-
panum. When a stick drawn was marked as a prize,
the drawer was entitled to a certain amount of the
contents of the pedlar's basket ; but if it was marked
as a blank, his money was lost. The first basket I saw
had a tray, with goose eggs, hard-boiled; salted duck
eggs, also hard-boiled ; sweet cakes; toffee; and peanuts. Some baskets had coloured tapes, used for tying
up Chinamen's gaiters ; buttons, and all sorts of nick-
nacks ; eatables being more plentiful than anything else.
What an appetite for gambling these men seem to
have! The Pekingese are the most noted gamblers in
China. Misery is always the result of their gambling.
Fortunes are lost and families ruined in their gambling
dens.

Rattle! rattle! rattle! half-a-dozen bamboos striking at once make quite a lively noise. Round and
round the inn-yard they move, till all the new-comers
have drawn several times, and all the cakes are gone.
The eggs also have disappeared. Indeed, the trays are
pretty well cleared out. It reminded me of what goes
on in some fancy bazaars at home, where fair young
ladies go round and tempt the unwary to dip into their
mystery bag, from which on payment of a sixpence one
may get something worth a penny. I think those

M

Chinese gentlemen fared better. They did look foolish drawing the sticks and getting a handful of peanuts as a reward. One unlucky wight drew a blank thrice, and he threw the stick into the man's face, and retreated into his room in disgust.

Meanwhile a brass basin filled with hot water is sent round, and every man washes his face in it. After the basin a teapot of large dimensions and cups to match were sent round with tea for the men. For an hour the inn-yard was lively, both with sound and motion. The mules were busily munching provender from mangers in the open air, three mules at each manger, each mule tied up short, so that if one felt greedy he could not · get more than his own share of grain or straw. The muleteers moved to and fro, adding now one kind of grain, now another, to the bait, which consisted of beans, black and green, Barbadoes millet, Indian corn, bran, and chopped straw.

Presently from the kitchen comes a waiter, bearing aloft a wooden tray, with four basins of meats and two plates of vegetables. There are two guests in each room. In a marvellously short time, each room has a second supply of four basins and two plates of vegetables. Little boys run in with bread steaming hot from the oven, and kettles with hot wine. The food looks palatable, and smells savoury : there are pork balls with mushrooms ; breasts of chickens with olives and vermicelli ; shrimps stewed with celery ; a white jelly with savoury sauce ; bean curd and onions ; kippered mackerel with garlic ; a nondescript dish of pigs' brains, with chickens' wings sticking out all over it, giving it a hedgehoggy appearance ; carp with onions ; a variety of vegetables ; tit-bits mostly condiments in small saucers ; ham sliced ; soup of chicken, flavoured with sorrel.

I was careful to get the bill of fare. That was not a despicable dinner for a country inn !

Bills all settled, purses all put up, guests crawl into their carts. Only one lady in Peking has the credit of

A CHINESE LIGHT CART OR CAB.

entering a cart with great dignity. Smack ! crack ! go the whips, as the carters gather up the reins. With an effort round go the heavy wheels, and out of the inn-yard they drive in most gallant style. As the carts pass my window I see that some of them are quite handsome, having coverings of blue cloth with arabesques of black

M 2

velvet relieved by white, decorated with a scarlet-and-white triangular flag. They are all armed. Two of them are particularly warlike, having each a ten foot spear, lashed obliquely to the side of the cart, and projecting over the heads of the animals. This spear has an old world look, with its lancewood shaft and glittering steel point. Just where the steel is inserted there is a long fringe of crimson silk, meant to represent dripping gore. In spite of the petticoats the men wore, the whole cavalcade had a martial look. We were constantly meeting such groups of travellers, varied occasionally by groups of officials. The latter are more imposing, but they usually have such a set of villainous-looking ragged followers that they are not so interesting as the every-day travellers.

After the departure of these gallants, silence falls on us. Every one has a siesta. Even our mules are nodding in the sun.

CHAPTER XXII.

The famine districts in Chih Li—Sad stories—A good dog story—
The departmental city of Ho kien foo—Roman Catholic
establishment and Church of England mission—The ruins of
old and handsome bridges—An inn three storeys deep—Sing-
song girls—A specimen of their musical recitations—Tune,
Madame Wang—Great distributing city of Ma Chow—A great
wholesale fair—Sign-boards and advertisements—A miserable
inn—The merrymaking of the fair—Canals and junks.

FOR two days we travelled over a district that had
suffered severely from famine. The tale was told in
roofless and doorless houses. All the woodwork had,
in many cases, been torn out and sold for food. The
millet stalks in the roofs had been taken and chewed,
to stay the pangs of hunger. In some villages many
houses were untenanted, and many fields around them
were untilled. The remaining inhabitants were finding
that in self-defence they would have to till these weedy
fields, as the seeds from thence were spoiling their good
crops. I asked where the people had gone from the
locked-up houses. 'Went away at the famine time,
and have not come back.' That was the invariable
answer. Still, the empty house is no proof that the
former inmates are dead; for they may have wandered
away, and found employment. Some day they may
return, and claim their houses and lands. In the hamlets, where the population was certainly greatly dimin-
ished, those that remained had a sturdy, healthy look.

In some places they offered their ground for sale at about ten shillings an acre. The soil had always been poor and dry.

Fever, too, had decimated these places. One great pile was shown where a whole family had died of fever. They had no one to bury them. A neighbour who had recovered from this famine fever went to see how they fared, and if he could do anything for them. He found the old grandmother seated on the doorstep, trying to call to some one who was staggering through a field. She entreated the neighbour to go and bring the man, for he was her youngest son. 'The rest are all dead,' she said, pointing to the two inner rooms. 'The baby was the last that died; it stopped crying this morning. I haven't yet gone in to see. I brought my darling boy out here, and now he has got up, and I can't follow him.' The man asked if she had food, 'Oh, yes!' she said, 'we have food, but we have fever too.' This kind neighbour went to get help, hoping to remove the old woman to a shed near. He returned with two men; but she would not let them come near till they went after her son. In a field at no great distance they found him, and carried him to her; he was dead. When she saw this the poor old woman gave one cry, and threw herself backwards over the door-sill. In a short time she also was dead.

It was evening when these two men left this sad house and went home. Next morning they reported the affair to the mandarin, who sent orders to have the house pulled down over the dead bodies. The men who had to fulfil the order stopped up their noses,[1] lifted the recently dead, and threw them beside the others.

[1] This is a common Chinese practice to avoid infection.

Then they pulled out all the large timbers, and pushed the whole structure in, and covered the corpses. This sad house-grave was shown to us. It stands on a little height outside the village. Near it, on the level road, was a well, nicely paved round. By order of the mandarin it had been filled up. Grass was plentifully growing from its mouth, which the paving stones defined. The whole story was sad and tragic. Such a story might be told of many villages, for 'The famine was sore in the land.'

Travelling on westwards, we passed a small plantation of trees. A good dog story is associated with it :—Many years ago, during the autumn, a pedestrian courier left Tsi-nan-foo on a journey to Peking. He had frequently made the journey to convey letters and money. On this journey he was entrusted with some small gold ingots. These were sewn into various parts of a wadded belt. He had agreed to reach Peking in a specified time under penalty for each day's delay. The man had a hardy collie dog as his companion in these journeys. Everything went prosperously until he reached this neighbourhood. In the evening, on arriving at one of the small inns, he missed his dog. He whistled, called, all in vain. He recollected that at a certain grove of trees where he had rested and had 'forty winks' his dog was with him. He had started up hurriedly, thinking he had lost time, and his dog was forgotten. Could doggie also have had 'forty winks' too many? The courier went to bed hoping that ere morning the dog would turn up. Morning came—no collie. On a former occasion the dog had hurt his foot, and of his own accord had gone straight home. So the man concluded that this time, also, on missing his master he had returned to his home.

Without his companion he felt lonely, but his letters admitted no delay. So on he trudged to Peking. When he reached the city his wadded belt was undone, one ingot was missing. How could this be ? In every direction the belt was felt, and finally cut to pieces. The place where the missing ingot had been was plainly seen. A defect in the seam of the belt showed where it had slipped out. The man's honesty was undoubted, evidently he had lost the gold. So he gave a mortgage on his farm in Shan-tung for the amount.

A storm of snow prevented his immediate return, so he took a position as a workman with the man whose money he had lost. When the severity of the winter was past he started homewards. On reaching this grove, a particularly lofty tree recalled it to his memory. Association of ideas made him look towards the tree under which he had slept. There was a heap of something. The fallen leaves had been whirled about, and in that place they made a little mound. The man walked straight over to the tree, kicked the leaves aside, and disclosed the remains of his lost favourite. ' Can he have become sick, and been unable to follow me ? ' said the man to himself. Immediately the lost ingot occurred to him. He removed the dog, and there lay the gold ! Gratitude and sorrow together made him go down on his knees and wail as one wails for an only son. He laid his dog in the centre of a triangle formed by three lofty trees, heaped a mound of earth over him, and half-grieving, half-joyous, retraced his steps to Peking.

The merchant whose gold he returned presented him with money enough to put up a tablet to commemorate the faithfulness of his canine friend. He also got imperial permission to erect the stone. The weather was too wet for me to hunt up the stone, even had I known the spot where to look for it.

Thirty li from Shen Kia Lin we reached Ho kien foo. The only interesting part of the road between the two places is that which lies along the new canal that has been dug to drain away the overflow of the waters of 'China's Sorrow.' The people repeatedly asserted that the seventy thousand men engaged in this work were fairly well paid. They further said that these workmen did not plunder, but paid for all they got. Their chief food was rice, brought along the canal in imperial junks. A great many soldiers were stationed at various points, to keep these navvies in order.

The wall of Ho kien foo is fine, and in thorough repair. The gateways are lofty, with a quadrangle and interior gate. In passing through to reach our inn at the western suburb, we found that the city looked desolate. Large portions of it were uninhabited. All the houses have flat roofs. Towards the western portion of the city we passed a lofty crenelated wall enclosing a good space of ground, with fine trees. We saw no buildings in the enclosure, but the people told me it was a *kiang shu tang*, or 'expounding books hall,' the name they usually give to a Christian temple. It was a Roman Catholic establishment. Both priests and converts were well reported of by the people.

In this neighbourhood, about two miles from the city, there is a station of the English Church Mission. The cook at the inn did me not a few kindnesses, because he said the Rev. W. H. Collins, of the Church Missionary Society, had cured his mother of ague, from which she had suffered for several years.

Just outside the west gate we crossed the Poo too river. The bridge, a handsome one, seemed very ancient, and on the four buttresses nearest the banks reposed four frogs in granite, with outspread feet, and a horrible grin, or leer, on their faces. On the east side of the bridge were the heads of two imperial tortoises. The slabs they had once supported were nowhere to be seen. The tortoises themselves were now under a mass of mud bricks enclosing a manure heap! A magnificent *pei-low* lay in ruins. The blocks of stone were immense. The carvings in relief had been fine. The square columns had tracery exceedingly like that on some of the old pillars represented by Squire [1] as having been found in the land of the Incas. At the foot of these pillars had stood the usual grotesque representations that would craze the most enthusiastic student of natural history, and perplex the most inveterate unraveller of heraldic mysteries. Small respect had been paid to fallen greatness, for I noticed more than one doorstep adorned by a slab from the monument. There are Goths and Vandals in all lands.

We put up at a pretty inn; in Chinese parlance— three storeys deep, that is, having three sets of rooms in three courtyards. We occupied the innermost one. The innkeeper was very busy.

There were numbers of sing-song girls going about. All the evening there was a constant twanging of a kind of guitar, as an accompaniment to a most unpleasant screeching. However, as I listened and got interested in the story the singer was telling, I found it less unpleasant than it seemed when first it caught my ear. Unlike most of their songs, it was in the

[1] Squire's *Peru*, pp. 385, 386.

colloquial dialect, and was quite intelligible to me. One singer, whose voice was not disagreeable, sang a verse, and at the end of each verse the whole company sang the chorus. The chorus after each verse was different, but at the last line there always occurred an expression equivalent to our 'Oh, dear! oh, dear! alas!' Between each verse was a part spoken by another voice in good contrast to the screaming treble.

It may interest my readers to have a rough translation of the song, which is very popular. It is called—

Madame Wang.

> Sáh tswong, sah tswong, wei ah !
> Ling shae ur kaw ting dang,
> Kao ur, wun shing shuae ah.
> Ling shae ur, Wang Ta Niang.

(*Spoken*) Wang Ta Niang Tsing mun dzo dsieh lian, kao tung shang liao.

(*Chorus*) Yih whoa, yih whoa, Heigh !

Dzoong yung ie, puh tao woa te ku fang te shang liao.

Yih whoa, yih whoa, Heigh !

The translation of this verse is :—

> Outside of the gauze-covered window a neighbour tapped,
> The maiden within said, ' Who is there ? '
> The voice replied, ' It is your neighbour, Wang Ta Niang.'

(*Spoken*) Madame Wang came in and sat on a high stool, Heigho ! You are unkind not to come often, Heigho !

(*Chorus*) Yih whoa, yih whoa, Heigh !

> Madame Wang opened the damask curtains,
> Inhaled the fragrance of the toilette perfumes,
> Turned down the red damask coverlet,
> And saw that the girl had wasted to a shadow, alas !
> Yih whoa, yih whoa, Heigh !

Well, miss, how have you been ?
I have no strength or spirit, and cannot take my rice or tea, alas !

Yih whoa, yih whoa, Heigh !

Shall I call a doctor?

> Oh no, do not call him, I don't want him,
> He will feel my pulse and sound me,
> I am afraid of feeling and sounding, alas!
> > Yih whoa, yih whoa, Heigh!

Shall I invite a Buddhist priest?

> Oh no, a Buddhist priest will only be jingling and banging,
> I am afraid of jingling and banging, alas!
> > Yih whoa, yih whoa, Heigh!

Shall I send a Lama priest for you?

> Oh no, a Lama will only sing and chant,
> I dislike singing and chanting, alas!
> > Yih whoa, yih whoa, Heigh!

You don't want this, and you don't want that. How did you become so ill?

> In the third month, in the third month,
> At the birthday of the flowers,
> When peach-blossoms open and willows are green,
> I met a young student taking a stroll.
> > Yih whoa, yih whoa, Heigh!

Spring stroll or not! What has that to do with you?

> He loves me, for I am beautiful,
> I love him, he is young and a student,
> And we exchanged a few words of love.
> > Yih whoa, yih whoa, Heigh!

Love or not love, are you not afraid your parents will know?

> My father is seventy-eight, my mother is deaf, and her eyes
> are blind,
> I am not afraid of either.
> > Yih whoa, yih whoa, Heigh!

Well now it is all told out, what is it you wish me to do?

> Oh, my godmother, Madame Wang!
> I kneel for you to arrange this matter,
> I am not betrothed, he is not betrothed,
> If you cannot betroth us, I shall die.
> > Yih whoa, yih whoa, Heigh!

MADAME WANG.

MASTER CHANG.

This song is popular, and, it is supposed, was written to show that even in China betrothal is often at the wish of both parties.

There is a corresponding song, in which a sm art young bachelor tries to cast ridicule on their system of betrothal. In this song the intended bridegroom, in a most comical style, gives a list of his possessions, and at the close of each verse the chorus is,

'Yet my friends desire to betroth me.'

His possessions are enumerated :-

'An inkstone with the corner broken; a teapot with a vagrant lid and an abbreviated spout; a hat with the crown worn out; a robe with almost all the sleeves gone; shoes with the toes destroyed, &c. &c., these are all I possess.

'Yet my friends are bent on betrothing me.'

Next morning we pushed on to Ma Chow, where annually in the fourth month a great market is held. We found the place as gay as rose-pink paper and beautifully written Chinese characters could make it. Every few feet along the pavement, there was firmly planted in the street a red board, intimating the locality from which the merchant had come, and the goods he

A CHINESE MERCHANT.

had for sale. This advertisement was generally supplemented by a model of the particular commodity to be found within. On all sides were gigantic fans blazing with gold; umbrellas in gorgeous scarlet; bales neatly done up in matting; all sorts of signs, reminding me of what was the admiration of my childhood—the gilded lamb that used to be displayed over the hosier's shop-door, or the gilt pot of the apothecary. Here also the medicine man had a gilded or brilliant pewter pot to tell his story. Advertising even at home could scarcely outdo this; all the old *pei-lows* in the centre of the town were placarded with crimson bills, some of them high up over the lintels of the great structure. There were 'Immense sacrifices,' 'Grand clearings out,' 'Must be sold off this month,' just as at home. One man intimated that his fans must all be sold off, as he must return with an immense variety of other goods. The word that we are so fond of using, as our most convenient generic term for articles of merchandise, 'things,' is translated by the Chinese *toong si*, i.e. 'easts and wests.'

In the centre of the town, our books were, as usual, laid down, and our cavalcade went in search of quarters, which were not easy to find, as all the better inns were full of traders and their goods.

The market here is very old. Small shopkeepers from long distances come to it to buy from the traders. These traders bring their wares from great distances to this place, which seems to have been chosen as a market-place because of the water communication to it from many parts of the empire.

The market had all the characteristics of such a market at home. There were the amusements which delighted our rustics some thirty years ago. The most popular were merry-go-rounds, loaded with laughing fliers, 'snatching a fearful joy,' and rejoicing in their flight. I heard one lad say as he dismounted, 'It is better than having wings.' 'I don't know that,' said his companion, and at once gave proof that his flight had not agreed with him. There were conjurors spinning basins on the points of chop-sticks, and making children disappear from under baskets, and a flower grow up instead.   There were Punch and Judy shows, exactly like our own, where a Chinese Punch was administering marital chastisement, and a Toby in a frill barked defiance at the crowd.   There were wrestlers with immense muscles, wandering minstrels, and the much-patronised story-teller.   There were the usual hubbub and noise of a fair, but not the rude jostling or horseplay that our rustics are apt to treat their neighbours to on such occasions.   Nor was any drunkenness visible. Opium-smoking there would be, but that refined vice seeks quiet and retirement.   All the fun of the fair was gradually brought to a standstill.

When my husband returned from his Bible-selling we loaded our mules and set off.   Our road lay along one of the waterways.   A fine embankment, nicely planted with willow trees, and a wide expanse of cool, clear water made a pleasant landscape.   Men were tracking their boats by ropes attached to the very top of the masts.   Some of the boats were of a hundred tons.   At one point was a bridge; what is to be done? The bridge is of stone, and, though the arch is lofty, that tall mast cannot go under it.   'Will they stop here?' thought I.   I was speedily answered.   The mast was lowered by a hinge, and was placed flat on the deck.   After the bridge was passed, the wind was fair, the mast was raised again, the sail was hoisted, and their brown wings bore them swiftly on.

The bridge was fine, and the embankment had great piles of wood driven in it to keep the earth from slipping. The wheat on either side of this river looked magnificent. There were pretty villages along the banks and number-

less sails were seen.   There must be a great traffic on
this stream.

The day was hot, and it was a relief at times to pass
under the cool cavernous gateways of the cities.   At
some points, where the water had inundated the land
for miles, the people had driven in stakes, and with
reeds and earth had constructed floating islands, where
vegetables were growing most luxuriantly.

All along our route we were charmed with familiar
birds; everywhere we met the common house-sparrow.
After passing the Yellow River, rooks with their boisterous caw entertained us almost every evening.   In
the early morning, we found numerous wood-peckers
tapping on the trunks of trees; and in many groves
the turtle-doves greeted us with their mournful notes;
whilst in the villages we found every description of
tame pigeons.

N

CHAPTER XXIII.

OUR road lay by the brink of a pretty winding river,
the T'sing Ho. It was so tempting that I left my
shendzle, and had a glorious walk by the river-side.
After the long dusty roads we had traversed, this made
me think of the River of Life that is in the midst of the
paradise of God, and of what it will be to us who are
weary with the heat and strife of this present world!

The shelving banks of the river were green to the
water's edge. As the tiny wavelets rippled along it was
like the soft murmur of a mother's song in the ear of a
sleepy babe. The splash and rush of the flat-bottomed
junks, as they came up from behind and swiftly passed
with their sails full, were pleasing to the ear. Occasionally we overtook rafts, some laden with slender
spars of red pine, and some with naturally grown hay-
forks of beautiful ash, and as beautifully fashioned as
though cut out by the hand. Many rafts were constructed entirely of large lumber. Every now and then

the river shallows, and an island divides the channel.
The sun is low and large in the west, and is tinting
river and sail and raft, and even the faces of the boatmen, with a rosy light, and making the eastern hills
look like gigantic piles of crumpled rose-leaves.

The sun is setting as we enter the busy town of
Pao Kow ho, and it is a *bustling place*. It is a *Ma
teu*. The term is almost untranslateable. It means
neither a city nor a town, neither a ferry nor a ford,
neither a jetty nor a bund, but something of all these.
The place is in reality an emporium where the merchandise is chiefly brought by junks. The words ' *Ma teu* '
literally mean ' horses' heads,' and the name is thought
to be derived from the Phœnician vessels, whose prows
were all adorned with a horse's head. The early intercourse China had with other nations is not yet thoroughly
known, and often the history of a Chinese word leads
to some long-forgotten facts in their wonderful national
story. The derivation of this name for these places of
trade may be fanciful, but is not in the least improbable,
for the rows of junks moored at such places must have
borne a striking resemblance to horses' heads.

We got to a fine inn, built round the sides of
a space of ground almost as large as a public square.
It was the hour when the lumbermen and ferrymen
were leaving their labour, and instead of going home
they streamed straight into the inn-yard. A wild and
turbulent set of fellows they seemed. The schools
were dismissing, and the schoolboys joined the throng
already in the spacious inn-yard. They were vociferously
shouting that foreigners had come, and looked inclined
for some rude horse-play. My husband had not quite
regained his vigour, and was scarcely able to address

such a mob. There were two immense gates to this inn-yard, and so soon as the bookseller could get them to reason at one side of the court, a fresh influx at the other upset his plans for quietness. Meanwhile my husband was busy at the front door selling books as fast as he could. I shall not soon forget the sound all this mob of men made.

All at once they left off their noisiness. A mandarin of the place, an old friend of my husband, sent his servants with his card, and an offer to do anything he could for us, also a request for certain books. The coming of the mandarin's servants put the people into order. My husband's Chinese name ran from mouth to mouth. The official lantern of the great man was enough to quiet the crowd, and afterwards only a few boys made any attempt to be noisy.

Here we noticed what is often the case as to Chinese rivers. The name given to this river by the townspeople was different from the name given to it along its course. The boatmen called it the Ta T'sing ho, 'Great Clear River,' while the townspeople called it 'White Dog River.' They had some fable about a dog, from which they named the part of the stream that flowed through the town Pao Kow ho. River and town had the same name.

A quiet night succeeded to a noisy evening. In the morning our start was too early for any idlers to be about. This time we made a false start, and found ourselves about a mile along the highway that leads direct to Pao ting foo, the capital city of the province of Chihli. Peking is in Chihli, but is the capital of the empire. We wished to take a road that would lead us through cities my husband had not previously visited.

CHINESE LUMBERMEN ON THE TA T'SING HO.
(*From a Chinese Engraving.*)

As I was trudging along well ahead of the cavalcade, I was startled by a cry to halt. Then the mules were driven in an opposite direction. I was not sorry we had to retrace our steps, as the new route took us through a good part of the town and along the bank of the river, amongst the extensive lumber yards. Here we saw wood of all sizes, from the enormous log fit for the mast of some immense junk to slender spars of red pine. There were also piles of bent wood prepared in the half-circles that are so much used for Chinese chairs, and stacks of hayforks, all of natural growth. Our friends the lumbermen were by this time too busy to trouble us. The boys were in school. So it was pleasant to go along the bank of the stream. Suddenly, in the distance, I descry three of my own countrymen. It must be so, for there they are in kilts and Scotch bonnets, hosen and brogues. Genuine Highland men they look, each bearing a net on his shoulder. A nearer inspection proved them to be only Alister MacAlisters in process of evolution. They were clad in fishers' garb. The kilt was of rushes; the wide hat had a red topknot. Their legs were bandaged in a crossway pattern, and they had coarse untanned pigskin shoes for brogues.

In the afternoon we reached the city of Tso Chow. We were much in need of a little rest and quietness. Like all Chinese cities, Tso Chow has a great street running east and west, and a corresponding one running north and south. It has lofty gates, an outer and inner, and is surrounded by great walls. The gates are surmounted by temples. The temples over the south gate of Tso Chow must have been beautifully decorated. Now they are shabby in paint and gilding. There was a central temple, in which the great idol sat in state. At either side was a shrine surmounted by a canopy supported by four massive pillars. It was something like the shrine that now covers the Pilgrim Rock at Plymouth. This, though smaller, was in form handsomer than the memorial of the Pilgrim Fathers. In the shrine to the east there hung a magnificent bell. The archways of the gates are very thick, strong, and wide. This strength is required to support the great mass of temple buildings above.

In the morning we discover that, though the nation has not changed her gods, she has changed her colours. The Eastern Empress is dead, and the land mourns. The last city through which we passed was all gay with scarlet. Now Tso Chow is in mourning. The outward and visible sign of this mourning is the suspension at every shop of two or more squares of blue stuff, satin, silk, or calico, according to the wealth or taste of the owner; but all

> ' In that deep-blue, melancholy dress
> Bokhara's maidens wear, in mindfulness
> Of friends or kindred dead.'

The crimson has always a gay and holiday look. The blue has a sombre hue, and is rather sad-looking.

The Empress was but a woman, yet in all this land, for a hundred days, while what is called ' heavy mourning ' lasts, no man may lift a razor, no man may shave either beard or head. During that time the barber's office is a sinecure, and he must live as best he may. Three days are allowed to prepare, and after that the Celestials go about looking simply horribly dirty. All officials change their cards, letter-paper, and envelopes. For the first twenty-seven days the cards, letters, and envelopes are of the colour of dead gold; the envelopes having a strip of the melancholy blue, pasted down. On this the name is written. At the end of twenty-seven days the officials change cards again, from old gold to a bright yellow, the letter-paper to green, and the envelopes to white with a red stripe. At the end of one hundred days the officials may return to the usual red card, the barber may again flourish his razor, and every Chinaman go back to his normal state. This mourning is a severe trial to the Chinese. My servant says, 'It feels dreadfully uncomfortable to have the head unshaven for such a length of time.' The Chinese have quite a tropical growth of hair—if that term may be applied to human heads.

The 'Peking Gazette' also is in 'heavy mourning,' with blue lines dividing the columns. All over the land there may not be any festivities. Any marriage that may have been arranged must either take place during the three days of preparation, or be delayed till the hundred days have expired.

For twenty-seven months also no theatres are allowed to be opened, and no plays to be performed in public. The religious festivals are not interfered with after the twenty-seven days of deep mourning have expired.

In going through the main street of Tso Chow, I was greatly interested by what the shopkeepers do to beautify the various devices by which they make known what they have for sale. A large tobacco pipe, elaborately carved and gilded, reposing in a gigantic satin-lined pipe-case, proclaims the tobacconist. A gilded boot needs no explanation. The money-changer tells his trade in strings of burnished 'cash,' pendant at either side of his shop. The mortar and pestle of our apothecary in England are represented by a brass canister with an ornamental lid, which the ‘medicine man’ displays. The three golden balls of Britain, upon which we look as the emblem of pawnbroking, are represented by a large black character on a white ground. The Chinese character *tang* is quite a handsome one. When anything special is going on in a shop, such as an auction, the proprietor places outside his door a tall pole of

THE CHINESE CHARACTER ‘ TANG,’ THE PAWNBROKER'S SIGN.

black and gold, with beautiful ornamental black and scarlet tassels.

The pawnshop of China is quite a reputable institution. It is more associated with banking than anything else. Almost all the banks have been pawning places; for as their business transactions increased they allowed the inconvenient pawn to lapse, or in most cases they limited the articles received to gold and silver and jadestone ornaments. A legal pawnshop has a government

licence. On receiving the licence, the owner also gets
a small sum of money as a loan. The *Mont-de-Piété*
of France more nearly resembles the Chinese mode than
the British ordinary pawnshop. The government at
present allows pawnbrokers to charge three per cent. a
month on small sums advanced, two and four-tenths per
cent. a month on large sums. This interest varies, but
the lowest interest allowed to be charged is one and six-
tenths per cent. a month. Large capital is required to
carry on this business, and government will not grant
licences except to wealthy individuals.

The articles pawned, unless redeemed, are kept, it is
said, for three years, but actually only *into* three years—
that is, for twenty-seven months. They are then sold
for the benefit of the establishment. A list of the
articles, with the names of the depositors, is posted up
some days before the sale, so that owners may have a
final opportunity to redeem their pledges. A really good
pawnshop, careful of its reputation, will give to a de-
positor any excess realised on the value of the pledge
he has been unable to redeem, if by any well-known
calamity, such as fire or loss at sea, he has been driven
to relieve temporary personal need.

These auctions are conducted in a most refined
manner. The Chinese call them 'Dumb Auctions.'
After the names of the depositors have been posted for
the legal time the goods are considered 'sealed,' and
cannot on any plea whatever be redeemed. All the
goods are laid out in lots for inspection. Intending
purchasers go in, examine the goods, and judge what
they are worth. Each purchaser writes on a slip of
paper his name and the price he is willing to pay for
the lot represented by a number. On the afternoon of

the same day the pawnbroker's assistant reads off the numbers of the lots that the head man is willing to dispose of. Very many of these silent bids are given for one article, which the highest bidder gets. If the pawnbroker thinks the offers do not come up to the value he declines to sell, but in that case there is no refusal, and the goods are again bidden for. Family valuables are often redeemed in this quiet way when some rascally member of the family has pledged them, and refused to give up the ticket.

Thieves and rogues of all kinds have a wholesome dread of these reputable establishments. They fear detection, and prefer to deal with small shops, whose owners are really receivers of stolen goods. Almost all these illegal pawnbroking places are in close proximity to opium dens. The rate of interest charged in them is exorbitantly high, but a great portion of the profit goes as bribes to mandarin runners, and constables who keep these receivers from being molested. To cover their illegal proceedings, these shops often are under the name of a widow with a number of fatherless children.

Sometimes most daring women lend their names, and give assistance to rogues generally. Some years ago at one of the ports a woman of this description hired herself to represent the widow of a man supposed to have been shot. Daily she appeared with a retinue all in mourning, and howled before the residence of the judge who had given an adverse decision. This continued so long that the judge got desperate, and ordered a detachment of marines to protect his house. The admiral realised the joke, sent a detachment of marines with thirty rounds of cartridges each, and orders to fire on the first woman they saw. Of course the joke was too broad; but the woman became a heroine because she had succeeded in causing so much annoyance to the representative of British law.

After this digression, I must return to my post on the street of Tso Chow. I observed a great many walls with the character *tang*. These places were surrounded by very high and strong walls, indeed there was no opening in them save the door, and the walls were decorated with placards containing long lists of pledges and their depositors. It was very early morning, yet the street was full of peripatetic kitchens, and scores of men were eating a delicious-looking white soup, into which they were sopping hot dough-nuts.

Outside the north gate of the town is a magnificent bridge of many spans. I counted three hundred small white marble pillars in the parapet; these pillars are divided by large slabs of stone of different sizes, some as large as five feet, while none are smaller than three feet. This shows the great length of the bridge. In two places it widens out into recesses. At one of those recesses were two elephants finely cut in white marble. Though under life-size, they were very imposing.

At the south end of the bridge there was an ornamental *pei-low*, or rather gateway. It was as brilliant as vermilion pillars and green and gold could make it. At either side were shrines with tablets standing on the imperial tortoise. These were all of very recent date. What a fitting heraldic emblem! While we for our royal arms have the fleet unicorn and the strong lion, slow-paced China chooses—what? a tortoise! The tortoise is chosen for its longevity.

At the north end of the bridge is a handsome canopy of wood, which at one time had been rich in colour with lacquer and paint and gilding. South of this canopy are eight immense blocks of white marble, with couching lions carved on the top. To the north are two very ancient and large bronze lions; but the casting is not fine, as the bodies are seamed all over like patchwork. This whole bridge is magnificent. As you stand in the centre, in one of these recesses, and look around, there is much beauty in the view. We saw it in the majestic glory of a gorgeous sunrise: the western hills tinted on one side rosy, and the shadows dark deep blue; whilst the lower hills, which the sun's rays had not touched, were dark, almost black. The still, smooth water, the vivid green of the banks, and the wheat-fields made a wealth of colouring that throws completely into the shade all the puny efforts of man. A little way off is another bridge older than that already noticed, and decayed. At the west end of this bridge stands an immense slab of black marble, perhaps over fifteen feet high, resting on an imperial tortoise, also of black marble, the whole very handsome, and worthy of an emperor. The temple in which it is enclosed is entirely of stone; even the balustrades that surround the slab are hewn in stone. These monuments are mostly old; many of them were gifts of the Emperor Kang Hi.

The people in this place must be tormented by wolves, for I saw in many places their walls marked with vivid white circles. They believe that these circles scare the wolves. How or when the wolves gave inti-mation of their feelings regarding these circles I have not ascertained; but one man told me he lost thirteen pigs through neglecting the circles, while not one of his neighbours who had the circles lost any—though they had more pigs, and fatter ones.

CHAPTER XXIV.

How our ' walking map' turned out—Difficulty of governing desperadoes—A run on a bank—The summary punishment of the
villains—An escape from roughs—A new feature on the ' old
highways'—Camels : their drivers and burdens—Approach to
Peking—Bad roads—A Peking street—The walls—Manchu
women—Origin of the small feet—Bandaging and the pain it
causes.

NOT long after leaving home we discovered that our
' walking map' had made good use of his opportunities.
In every district through which he had passed he seems
to have acquired any wickedness that might be new
and fashionable, and he grew especially proficient in
the art of harassing his unfortunate travellers.   He
was, as all bullies are, a coward, for if we were near a
magistrate's bureau he was as respectful and honest as
possible ; but when we came to caravanseries, and where
the scum of the cities had collected, he was quite un-
bearable.   He drank and gambled, and when anxious
to show off before the roughs he was something fearful.
He always carried an open knife in his sleeve, and
threatened all who displeased him.   He was, without
exception, the worst muleteer we ever travelled with.

Only the utmost forbearance on the part of my
husband, and a complete knowledge of the rules of the
road, enabled us to get along in safety.   The roughs

instinctively recognised the man who was neither going to be plundered nor frightened.

Our experiences with that muleteer made me pity mandarins who have to take charge of such ruffians; and one can scarcely be surprised that capital punishment is so often resorted to in order to keep such scoundrels in awe. These villains are not simply brutish. They are astute, keen-minded men, and therefore can do much mischief.

Lately, in a great city, a group of such desperadoes, in revenge for some deduction of cash, resolved to harass a large and honourable native banking company. They laid their plans widely and carefully, and they succeeded in making such a run on the bank that the city was in danger. The mandarin at once, and most unexpectedly, seized one or two of the ringleaders, and, after showing clearly that they were the cause of this uproar, decapitated them. In one hour the town was quiet, and there was not a rough left. They saw where the power lay, and took the hint to decamp and preserve their heads.

I once had a long talk with a mandarin on the rapidity with which they hurry on trials and inflict capital punishment.

He said, 'These trials are all regulated by law, and those men know quite well when they make themselves liable to be taken up. Soldiers also know their code of military discipline, and it would be dangerous to let certain acts pass.' He said further, 'We have to rule in our own way and with our own weapons, else there would be no government.' He said that there is no law for a mandarin to decapitate ruffians when they raise mobs against foreigners. Hence the Tien-tsin massacre. Had the women massacred there been Chinese subjects, H. E.

Chang-How could legally have decapitated the ringleaders in the street, but he had no law for that case, and had to wait instructions from the capital, the complaint requiring to be made by the British Minister.

At a small town forty li from Peking we spent the night. Early in the morning we started, and found the main street a quagmire, and as the feet of our mules dragged through it an almost intolerable stench arose. The inhabitants had a most dissipated appearance. They looked like the ruffians from a large city. I believe they were chased out of the capital, and had congregated here. Our muleteers seemed desirous of hobnobbing with these fellows. As we were leaving the inn there was a very faint attempt at a hoot, speedily suppressed by the innkeeper, for which I believe we were indebted to the ' walking map.'

All along the pathway were camels crouching, and as we left the street and climbed a bleak and stony ridge, we met strings of them moving with a slow, sailing motion. Ghost-like they were, with their great spongy feet and noiseless tread. They were in a very ragged state of coat, and did not appear to be respectable members of the animal kingdom.

These camels are chiefly used for conveying coal from the mines, and they must have become perfectly acclimatised. We passed hundreds of them. In the beginning of June they are driven off to the Mongolian plains, where they graze till September, as they cannot endure the heat of the city in summer. They are double-humped, very large, and shaggy in coat. Each has a saddle that goes completely round both humps, with a broad portion as a strap between them. They crouch to be laden, and the Chinese do not overburden them.

Amongst the hundreds we met I did not hear a sound uttered. The men who attend them are very few compared with those who drive other beasts of burden. I do not think the average was two men to twenty-five camels. These men usually ride the leaders. The camels are attached to each other by a string passed through a hole pierced in the nostril. It seemed a cruel fashion, but there is a liberal allowance of string, and they walk with so much regularity that I do not think they suffer. Besides, the end of the string is fastened to a guard of fine smooth boxwood. I only saw one camel with his nostrils slightly bleeding. The near camel of the string has a bell on his neck. This bell gives a hollow tum-tum sound, not a tinkle, like the bells on mules or horses.

In one of the sandy lanes, at a good distance from Peking, we met a string of camels carrying grain. They were very large, and seemed much better cared for than those laden with coal. They had long beards and bushy knee-pads. A mass of whity-brown hair on their heads reminded me of the Soumalis at Aden. Following this string there was a little foal. It was of a lovely fawn-colour, smooth and soft. Its little humps were beautified with a tiny mop of flaxen hair. As it gambolled round its dam, it was in great contrast to the tattered coat that she displayed.

Unused to such sights, our Shan-tung mules became troublesome, and one had to have his eyes covered. Although we met these camels during part of two days, the mules did not get reconciled to them, but always eyed them with suspicion, and made ready for a bolt.

The camel-drivers looked a stupid set of men. Their favourite dress was a long ulster, cut from one sheet of fine white felt sewn with brown twine, a seam up each

side under the arm and down the sleeve. When it rains
the camels have each a large sheet of matting girthed
over their burdens, and almost covering the whole body.

String after string of camels are seen, more numerous
and more ghost-like as we near the wondrous city of
Peking, whose walls loom up before us in the grey of a
drizzly morning. Grand and imposing the gate looks,
fit entrance to this city of the Celestials; but, alas for
our enthusiasm! we have to pass over a miry road full of
ruts, in which the mules find such unsafe footing as to
render us apprehensive of 'a spill.' When a shendzle
falls it is literally a spill, as I once experienced.
When travelling during the night, the front animal took
fright at the muleteer striking a match, backed, and by
his pressure on the long poles threw the hind mule off
the path. Over went the shendzle, down a deep ravine,
roll, bump, over and over; and with each turn a shower
of books, tins, cups, spoons, and finally a sprinkling of
such groceries as remained after a long journey, over-
whelmed the unfortunate occupant.

The remembrance of that memorable night kept me
intent upon maintaining the proper balance of the
shendzle, as I saw a chance of my being upset into
some odious cesspool, or submerged in a duckweedy
ditch, half sewer and half canal.

However, in time we safely passed the ditches that
abound in the neighbourhood outside the city wall, and
reached the paved road that leads to one of the western
gates. A well-paved avenue it had once been, but now
in some places the immense blocks of stone are worn
into deep ruts by the ceaseless traffic; in other places
the stones have been removed, giving rise to the suspicion that the neighbouring householders have helped

themselves to these fragments of imperial property. For many of the mud-holes in front of the houses are provided with a stone crossing, whose likeness to the stones of the avenue is too evident. Along each side of this paved way there is a deep fosse, and the remains of a row of trees.

The road presented a curious scene. The middle of it was filled with carts of various sizes, some immensely large, drawn by many-coloured teams, consisting of from seven to fourteen mules, donkeys, and horses. Others were the carts of gentlemen, drawn by one large and handsome mule. There were also costermongers' carts, wheelbarrows of all descriptions, and our shendzles made a picturesque addition to the vehicles.

The unpaved side-paths are taken possession of by the camels, some strings of them laden with coal, others with lime, entering the city on the one side-path; while those rid of their loads, and returning to the mines or lime pits, as the case may be, are filing down the other pathway. Pedestrians get along as best they can, picking cut the driest stones, and displaying an amusing variety of pattern in umbrellas. Here and there boys are amusing themselves by splashing in the pools of water, others are offering small donkeys for hire to the unfortunate pedestrians.

The road is so crowded that we are obliged to go slowly, and thus have ample time to see that the city lies on a sloping plain, the Si Shan, or western hills, forming a fine approach to this side of the city.

The wall is about 40 feet high, 62 feet thick at the base, and 34 feet at the top. Massive buttresses are thrown out at intervals. All the wall is crenelated, and has a great many embrasures for cannon. Over each gate there is a lofty tower, and as we approached our muleteer declared the tower was a hundred feet high. The exact measurement is ninety-nine Chinese feet. These towers have a most imposing look, and I do not wonder that the Chinese are proud of their capital.

As we passed through the tunnel formed by the gateway we could not but admire its solid strength, and the semicircular *enceinte* adds to the effect. As a defence, the wall of Peking is not contemptible. It is well known that in 1860, when one of the city gates was in possession of the French and English troops, the officers who examined the massive thickness of the walls were not quite certain that they would have been able to batter them down; at least, in their opinion it would have been somewhat difficult.

It was not only in passing through it that we admired it, but subsequently, when we walked up one of the inclined slopes that lead to the platform on the top, we found it well paved, handsome, and wide ; the whole in the most perfect order, with abundant gutters to lead the water off. What a splendid promenade it was ! and from it we had a most extensive view of the city. The yellow of the imperial roofs, the green-tiled roofs of the princes, the number and variety of the buildings, and the foliage of the trees, made a most pleasing picture.

In the streets of the city my notice was at once attracted to the Manchu women, walking about with feet of the natural size. Accustomed to the miserable gait of the Chinese women, I could not but admire the grace of their movements. So many of these women were going about, that it seemed as if we had left ' little-footed China ' outside the walls of Peking.

The persistency of Chinese women in cramping their feet is a familiar instance of how far fashion can make deformity popular. This practice took many centuries to gain favour and arrive at its present universality. The best authorities state, and all the information I can gain on the subject shows, that this custom is simply fashion. The practice began A.D. 501. An empress called Pan Fei, to whom nature had granted exceedingly small feet, was accustomed to show their beauty by walking over a platform covered with crimson cloth, embroidered with golden lilies. The emperor used to say, 'Each footstep made a lily grow'; so that the little feet of the women are called 'golden lilies.' The ladies tried to rival Pan Fei's feet by bandaging their own. This fashion took a long time to become popular. In A.D. 975, the last empress of the famous Tang dynasty, who was the most beautiful woman of her time, had clubbed feet. She bandaged and ornamented them so successfully that the fashion of cramped feet spread through the whole empire. The Emperor Kang-Hi, the founder of the present Manchu dynasty, in 1662 made a great effort to suppress footbinding. After issuing one edict that proved ineffectual, he prepared another, accompanied with most stringent and severe penalties; but his advisers warned him that if he persisted it would probably cause a rebellion. Thus the conquerors of China were conquered by the women of China. They set their tiny feet on princes! On the men he imposed the shaven head and the queue, and also the dress they were to wear; but when he tried to suppress this practice the women defied him.

The fact that all the empresses of the Manchu dynasty have large feet is too frequently overlooked.

Another anomaly in this empire, where so many customs are contrary to Western lands, is that whereas royalty in Europe leads the fashion, here it fails, and the *pei sing,* the 'hundred families,' carry the day according to their own whims.

A most serious whim this is. The process begins in the child's fifth year. The little foot is taken by the mother, the four toes, leaving the great toe free, are pressed down completely under the sole : a bandage seven feet long and about an inch and a half wide is used. This bandage is wound over the toes, and crossing the foot is passed round the heel. The strength of one woman is not considered sufficient, so another stands behind and pulls at the bandage. It is wound over the toes and around the heel till the whole seven feet of cloth is expended. This bandage is tightened day by day till the foot acquires the desired shape and smallness. The process is continued for years, and the pressure is never relaxed.

There are three degrees of compression. The first is adopted by some of the very poor peasant women, who expect their daughters to have hard work, when the foot is not quite destroyed. The second degree is most common, and in Shan-tung almost every woman of the middle class, and many of the poor, endure it. The bandage is drawn so tight as to make the foot a shapeless mass; the toes are so pressed into the sole as almost to obliterate them, unless, indeed, they become diseased and require treatment. The third degree is not often practised. In this case the foot is desired to be so small that the great toe is also curved down under the sole.

This cramping entails great suffering. I have

always found the little feet hot and painful till the girl has attained her full growth. While some women say that they did not experience much pain, most tell me that at intervals it was excruciating torture. I have often found young girls rocking themselves to and fro, evidently in extreme suffering because of the bandage.

Besides in many ways destroying the health it shrivels the leg, and often produces serious disease in the foot itself. Diseased bone in the instep has often been treated in the hospital at Chefoo. Sometimes the toes fester. Frequently women would come to the hospital suffering so much that they implored me to amputate the painful toes. After a while, finding they could thus obtain relief from pain, they came in great numbers.

Notwithstanding this pain and deformity, I have found it a most difficult subject with which to deal. When I have proposed to undo the bandage to give relief, even very little girls would refuse, and say, ' Oh, no ! we could not let you do so. We should not be fit to be seen.' Those little feet ! the one vanity of the Chinese women. They are not vain of their beautiful hair or of their lovely complexions, but these tiny feet and exquisitely embroidered shoes occupy their whole thoughts. Strange that they should be vain of such folly, for as the women get old there is something perfectly repulsive in the look of these cramped, disfigured feet. At all times their gait in walking is simply a kind of totter. Yet we find it a matter we can hardly touch, and as it does not involve a question of morality, we must trust to gradual enlightenment and to the spread of Christian principles.

Passing through Peking, we were charmed by the gay appearance of everything. We pushed slowly on, and after traversing miles of streets, passing legation after legation, we arrived at the premises of the National Bible Society of Scotland, where we stayed.

CHAPTER XXV.

Peking—Its plan, buildings, and institutions—Its social economy—
Improvements since 1866—Railway and telegraph—Journey by
canal—Infanticide not common in North China—Tien-tsin—The
Pei ho—The Taku Forts—Chefoo.

PEKING is a twin city: the Tartar portion on the
north, a square, three miles each side : the Chinese
city on the south, an oblong, nearly five miles by two.
Originally it must have been a splendid city, lying
as it does on a gentle slope, and built upon a most
enlightened plan. It is a city of parallelograms, with
spacious streets cutting each other at right angles. It
has an abundant and never-failing water supply from the
western hills, large lakes, a canal running through the
city, and a good system of drainage. Notwithstanding
its present dust, dirt, dilapidation, and cesspools, it
might be made one of the most beautiful capitals.
Were due advantage taken of the several rivers which
rise in the semicircle of hills on the north-west, avenues
of trees might shade each side of the thoroughfares,
and there might be running streams on both sides of
the streets.

It is a most interesting city still, with its elegant
Prospect Hill in the centre, adorned with clumps of
shady trees and numerous arbours. The imperial palaces,

the palatial residences, the handsome legations, the altar
to the Most High God, on which, every year at the
winter solstice, a red heifer, without blemish and without spot, on whose neck the yoke has never passed, is
most devoutly offered as a whole burnt offering—the
most ancient and continuously offered religious rite that
has ever existed in the world—all impress the traveller.
He gazes wonderingly at the elegant triple-roofed
dome of glistening blue raised in honour of Heaven,
with its ancient cult, and within whose glass venetians
of sapphire blue there stands no idol, but only a tablet
to the Supreme Ruler of the universe; at its great
reception halls, its ornamental gateways, its pagodas, and
dagobas, bell and drum towers for time and fire signals.
He meets with much to interest him at the altar to
Earth, at the temples to the Sun and Moon, and the
shrine to Agriculture. The Lama University, with its
four courses of study, and its resident students (Lamas),
ranging from thirteen to fifteen hundred; its morning
devotions, with its gorgeous ritual and wondrous deep
bass music. Then there are the Hanlin College, or
Imperial Academy, the College of Medicine, government schools where young men designed as inter-
preters are taught Manchu, Mongol, Thibetan, Cochin-
Chinese, Turkish, and, formerly, the Burmese and
Newara languages. These are now all eclipsed by the
Tung Wen Kwan (Peking College), where the chief
European languages are taught, and the various
sciences of the West. There are also carefully kept
imperial libraries, the catalogue of one alone occupying
two hundred volumes.

Peking also presents a splendid field for the archæo-
logist: many of its most famous sacred and imperial

buildings being fac-similes of ancient structures dating, from B.C. 1200 to B.C. 800, abounding in relics of all descriptions, such as the stone drums, possessing a history of 2,500 years; the eleven bells of the Chow dynasty, B.C. 1200 to B.C. 220; the eighteen tripods, the standard measure of capacity, and imperial dial; the famous gallery of portraits of all the emperors and empresses, and all the noted statesmen and learned men, from the earliest historic times to the present day.

There are trilingual and tetralingual marble slabs; huge printing offices, where the imperial almanac is printed yearly in three languages—Manchu, Mongol, and Chinese; the court from whence the daily newspaper, called the 'Peking Gazette,' has for centuries been distributed by swift couriers all over the empire, where it is reprinted; the six boards, dating from a most early period : viz. the Boards of Civil Office, of Revenue, of Rites, of War, of Works, and of Punishments; the Tsungli Ya Men, or Foreign Office. In addition we have survivals of customs of the deepest interest to the antiquarian.

No less interesting to the student of human nature are its varied industries. Its Paternoster Row, where there are huge book-stores with books marvellous for size; national histories and geographies, which for fulness and accuracy entirely eclipse all other nations. There are also all the trades necessary to civilisation—workers in metal, pewter, brass, iron. There are places where carts stand for hire, not unlike the cab-stands of London. There are many objects of interest in the social economy of the city—its system of police, its system of lighting, perfect in theory, its fire and time signal towers; its clubs, where literary men have their wine parties, and wit flashes freely; its caravanserais, restaurants of wondrous size ; its encampments of the various nationalities of the East, such as the Mongol encampment, the Thibetan, the Corean, the Loo-chooan, the Cochin-Chinese, Burmese, and the Nepaulese, with their diverse costumes and equipages which make Peking unique among the cities of the East.

Then there are the tremendous granaries, the residences of the Manchus of the eight banners, and the various Mongol banners.

Nor are these people wholly material; they have spiritualistic halls, where séances are held, spirit-rapping, spirit-writing, volumes of poetry written by spirits, astrology, divination, jugglery, and all the occult sciences so much prized by those whose minds are dark and unrestful.

There are also benevolent and charitable institutions, such as foundling hospitals, asylums for the blind, hospitals for the relief of the aged, and a dispensary for coffins for the poor. These institutions may not be so efficiently carried out as one could wish, but the germ is there, and is a proof of the considerate and liberal character of the Chinese.

On this occasion I observed many signs of manifest improvement since my last visit in 1866. There were gas-works erected by the Inspector-General, which now light up the premises of the Imperial Customs. There was a brisker trade, and the shops were in better order, both as to stock and decoration. There were fewer uninhabited houses, and many more dwellings were in process of repair. This process of renovation will probably go on, and while these pages are passing through the press news has reached us of old prejudices giving way. Railways have been publicly and officially sanctioned by the Government, and there is a probability of two great trunk lines being laid, one from Peking to Canton, the other from Shanghai to North-west China. The world-wide network of telegraphy has already thrown its first two lines into the city of Peking, one for official de-spatches into the Tartar city, the other for business pur-poses into the Chinese city.

We dismissed our shendzles at Peking, and after spending some time there, started homewards *viâ* the canal and the Pei hoh River. A kind friend lent me a sedan chair, as we had former experiences of the miseries of being jolted over the twelve miles of paved avenue that lie between the city gate of Peking and Tung Chow, where we hired a boat.

We found the dust a serious inconvenience, but our coolies were stalwart fellows, and marched along at a rapid rate. These men declared to me, and persisted in the speech, that they could walk faster with the chair than without it, as the impetus of the chair swung them along. Four coolies we had, and they carried by turns. They brought two tiny donkeys, and rode them when relieved from the chair.

I was alone, and the coolies made an attempt at being most polite and considerate. Wherever they stopped to drink tea they invariably brought out in a fine porcelain cup tea for the lady, and refused to take payment; so I in my turn invested in some tempting-looking cakes for the benefit of the party, and we had quite a sociable time.

We reached the canal, and here left the 'old high-ways.' There was no difficulty in hiring a boat; the trouble was to get it started. The boatmen promised to set off in the afternoon, but by various manœuvres they managed to detain us. There seemed no hope of

getting the crew together : first one man was missing—
' Oh, he had gone to purchase vegetables ' ; then another
went in search of him ; finally the missing man returned,
but the searcher did not, and a third man disappeared,
so they detained us till the morning. I did not regret
the detention, as I made friends with the women and
children in the neighbouring boats. On very many of the
boats there were whole families living. Healthy, happy-
looking children were plentiful, their mothers evidently
proud when the little ones were talked to. Domestic
discipline also was occasionally administered as the
bairns refused to go to sleep ; and no wonder, for few of
them had seen a foreign lady. Infant Celestials are not
as a rule cherubic, but sunny infancy is sweet all the
world over.

I have often been questioned as to the prevalence of
infanticide. In the north of China I have not found
any organised infanticide, and I have found parents
making most heroic efforts to bring up their little ones.
I have come on cases of mothers dying and leaving infants who I fear got small chance of living from their
relatives. Among all the women I have questioned in
Shan-tung only one confessed to having destroyed her
infant, a girl, and she did so to leave herself free to become a wet-nurse. Of the native women admitted to the
Church, not one had a tale of infanticide to regret, though
many with tearful eyes spoke of having lost three, four,
and five children by that dreadful scourge, small-pox.

The idea of infanticide is developed by the fact that
the Chinese believe that a child dying young has no
personal soul, and is only inhabited by a vagrant soul.
The officers of justice from Hades come and capture the
runaway spirit ; hence when a child dies under two

years of age they take no thought for the poor little
body; it is not interred in the family burying-ground,
but generally given to some coolie, who for forty cash
(about twopence English) promises to put it away; and
I know of two cases when the faithless, opium-smoking
fellow laid the little body down on a dust-heap close by.
Those who have travelled widely and mingled with
Chinese most intimately in North China, found that it
was not practised there. It unfortunately existed on some
parts of the seaboard which were first known to the outer
world, and hence the idea that the crime was prevalent
all over China. We all know that it was our blessed
Saviour who made infant life sacred when ' He took the
little ones in His arms, put His hands on them, and
blessed them'; and where His love is unknown the care
for childhood is not very active. The educated Chinese
are ashamed of infanticide, and in almost every city
have provided foundling hospitals; and also to relieve
the poor of the expense of interment the Government
provides towers outside of cities where dead infants
may be placed.

After all the infant laughter and tears had been
quieted we sat on the prow of our boat and enjoyed the
glorious moonlight; we admired the picturesque groups
of boatmen seated round their blazing fires, where in
immense caldrons the supper was being prepared, and
was ladled out hot and steaming; very palatable it
looked. A Chinaman is careful to have his meals comfortable, and has a horror of cold victuals.

In the morning there came the stir of unmooring
and getting out from the numerous boats around us.
Those remaining were very apathetic, and not in the least
inclined to assist those who were endeavouring to get out
of the maze. Amid many threats by the boatmen to cut

ropes unless they were pulled up, and a good deal of scolding, we at last got into the open stream, and were among the first of a long string of these river boats. We had the wind against us, so our progress was slow; however, we were repaid for this by being fortunate enough to meet a squadron of junks conveying a portion of the Government rice to Peking. They passed us at full sail, and it was really a fine sight to see the whole fleet as we did on that lovely summer day. We glided along the canal, made romantic by the name of Kublai Khan, and by all the pleasant memories of his capital, the old-world Kambalu. It seemed to me, after the fatigues of the shendzle, to be almost the perfection of travelling, to sit sheltered from the sun, yet able to view all that is going on as junk after junk in full sail passed, up the river.

All the way to the city of Tien-tsin these grain junks passed as close to each other as they could sail with safety.

Tien-tsin is a large and very busy city, reported to be the refuge of the offscourings of the capital, scoundrels who find it inconvenient to be too near the seat of law and order.

Tien-tsin is also of unenviable fame in regard to the sad massacre of the sisters of mercy and other foreigners in 1870. Here there is a Chinese arsenal, superintended by foreigners, gas-works, &c. It is also the head-quarters of his Excellency Li Hung Chung, the most notable man in China, the man who best understands the strength and the weakness of the empire.

About a mile from the native city of Tien-tsin is the foreign settlement, a pleasant place, well laid out with good roads and a handsome esplanade, or what in China is called a 'bund,' nicely planted with trees.

P

We found we were just in time to catch our favourite steamer, the *Sin Nan Zing*. Here we were in civilisation as to the steamer; but the river is so narrow and so winding that the first thing done after we got on board was to turn her round by means of a rope fastened to a post on the opposite side of the river; and funny she looked, with her stem and stern straight across the stream. Bend after bend we reach in the river, and always the same process is repeated : by means of a rope and a post on shore the steamer is twisted round to face down the stream.

A very little trouble would straighten and deepen the Pei ho, but the Chinese know that it is not in their interest to render their capital easy of access. One high official, a marine mandarin, told me that ' each bend in that river was worth a couple of ironclads to the Chinese Government.' And until justice rules the world, or, what will sooner come, until China has a navy that can cope with all the Western Powers, she wisely keeps her Pei ho's bends and double-bends. The ironclads she is rich enough to buy, but what years it will take ere she can have sailors and marines with bone and muscle hardened, and hearts made brave enough to get the title that our seamen rejoice in!

The winding course of the river had caused so many detentions that we were afraid of being too late to cross the Taku bar, where the celebrated fights took place in 1858–60. Ultimately the forts were captured by the allied forces, but afterwards returned to the Chinese. These forts are now repaired, and said to be very strong —the best national defences the Chinese possess—of far greater importance than the forts of the Min River at Foochow, or the Woosung forts near the mouth of the

Shanghai River. Off the Taku forts were lying several beautiful little gun-boats, the first of what is now called the Alphabetical fleet, they being named by the letters of the Greek alphabet. I suppose these must have been Alpha, Beta, &c. They are beautifully fitted, painted white, and rested on the water like gigantic sea-birds. These vessels are most valuable, as they carry good guns, and are in every way adapted for the shallow bays and rivers on the Chinese coast.

Passing the Custom House we reached the bar, fortunately just in time to get across, although, by the mud we stirred up, I believe our worthy captain brought his steamer partly over-land. Two larger steamers were lying, one outside the bar coming up the river, the other inside the bar going down. We left them there, smiling at each other like rival beauties.

This bar is a great grievance to the mercantile community in the coasting trade. Very little work, they say, with a dredger would keep a clear channel, as the bar is only the deposit from the river and the silt of sand from the tide. The Chinese, however, are not unmindful that vessels other than the valuable merchantman would find a ready passage; while with the bar, guarded by the Taku forts, nations who are fond of removing their neighbours' landmarks would take some time for consideration ere they would risk a run to Peking. The Mian Tau Islands lay brightened by the morning sun as we passed, and Chefoo Bluff looked its best as we again neared Chefoo, and recognised the old familiar smoke-tower.